How To Make A Solid Profit in the Apartment Business Year After Year

How To Make A Solid Profit in the Apartment Business Year After Year

. . . featuring the TAC* Principal

by

Joseph Schwartz

*Tenants Are Customers

FARNSWORTH PUBLISHING COMPANY, INC.
Rockville Centre, New York 11570

The author accepts no responsibility for the legality of any forms as laws and interpretations differ in many states. They are furnished for information and guidance only.

Joseph Schwartz

©1974, Joseph Schwartz.
All rights reserved.
First printing, 1974.
Second printing, 1975.
Third printing, 1976.
Fourth printing, March, 1977.
Fifth printing, November, 1977.
Published by Farnsworth Publishing Co., Inc.
Rockville Centre, N.Y. 11570.
Library of Congress Catalog Card No. 74-84338.
ISBN 0-87863-055-4.
Manufactured in the United States of America.

FOREWORD

Some months back Joe Schwartz walked into our association's offices to clarify some matter pertaining to his membership (which I have long since forgotten). In the course of our discussion he revealed to me that he was in the process of completing a book for landlords and would-be landlords giving some unorthodox advice on how to keep the "For Rent" sign away from their door.

"Would you like to review the manuscript when I complete it? I'd appreciate your opinion." How do you say "no" to an association member, particularly one as ingratiating as Joe Schwartz. I agreed to do so, half-hoping that the matter would be forgotten by the time the manuscript was completed—if it ever was.

Less than one week later—you guessed it—there was the manuscript deposited at my desk by the smiling author himself. I promised to review it as rapidly as I could and get back to him within a week or two.

When he left the office, I looked over the chapter headings and was intrigued by what was obviously some highly original thinking about the role of the landlord and what he should be doing to make a success of it, not just financially but as a member of society.

Before the day was out I had read the book. Thus I was privileged to be not only the first person to read it in its original manuscript form, but the first critic to give it a rave review.

Why do I think so highly of Joe Schwartz's remarkable book? Because its theme and its development are so unique.

Because it differs substantially (and in its favor) from so many of the other books I have read about the rental business. Because it gives so much valuable information and advice in a manner simple to understand and to follow. Because—and this is crucial—it is *not* just about *landlords* and their *tenants*. It is about *businessmen* and their *customers*.

The book, in short, doesn't just tell it as it is—it tells how it ought to be. It points out in an entertaining, engrossing style a new approach to owning apartments, and keeping them in full occupancy.

In breaking new ground in an area badly in need of new ideas, Joe Schwartz has charted a road map for the rental industry. Predictably some will scoff at some of the new-fangled notions. It's not easy to break old habits. Others—and I hope you are among them—will give the author-landlord serious consideration. If you do you will be the beneficiary of a great idea whose time has come.

—Howard Jarvis
Apartment Association of
Los Angeles County, Inc.

Howard Jarvis, well known in politics and government, is the Executive Director of the Apartment Association of Los Angeles County, one of the largest apartment house associations in the country.

He has had a distinguished career as a newspaper publisher, radio station owner, airplane parts manufacturer and apartment owner.

Mr. Jarvis is an outstanding advocate of tax reform, especially property tax revision, and is an acknowledged expert in the field.

A well known speaker, Mr. Jarvis has appeared before audiences in many parts of the country and on hundreds of radio and television programs. Since he became its Executive Director in 1972, the Los Angeles Association has tripled in size.

In commenting upon this book Mr. Jarvis said "the rental industry has become the most important service industry in the United States. It serves more people than any other industry. It must make a reasonable profit to survive and this book will help it accomplish these ends."

PROLOGUE

I have never been able to find any income property text-books for the individual, like myself, who owns small apartment buildings, perhaps just one or two. Therefore, this book was written to fill the need for such a business manual. Present owners should find it useful as an operational guide providing more satisfaction and profit. And, for the many would-be apartment house owners—this manual should help them decide whether or not this is a business that might be to their liking.

What's the big deal? Writing an apartment building text-book is about as earth-shaking as writing about gas stations, or shoe stores. So I would like to list four reasons for this "big deal":

1. To my knowledge, this is the first down-to-earth treatise of both sides (landlord and tenant) of this subject.

2. Thousands of people who now own apartment buildings shouldn't; many who do not should. This book will help the wrong ones out and the right ones in. In fact, it might even right some of the wrongs.

3. Condominiums—there is excellent material available on this relatively new, glamorous subject, but in the main, it is all pro—and it scares the hell out of apartment building owners. This book will not dwell on the minuses of condominiums but will add much to the plus side of the apartment building owners' ledger.

4. Most "tax shelter" owners will want to sell when the tax laws remove the shelter advantage. With thousands of buildings for sale at the same time, it will be a buyer's market. A WHO, HOW, AND WHAT TO BUY book is necessary.

TABLE OF CONTENTS

Chapter I

THE APARTMENT BUSINESS

or

sooner or later

I have discovered a new career—exciting, profitable, and essential—meeting an important social need. I am referring to the much maligned business of owning and operating apartment buildings.

Ownership alone does not earn the superlatives I have attributed to the apartment business—it requires proper operation also. Ownership is simple—anyone with money can be an owner. But the proper operation of the building is much more exacting. With proper operation the owner has a fool-proof investment, better than gold, silver, or the collection of fine arts, to weather the constant erosion caused by the endless inflationary trend.

But there is a way for those living on fixed income to hedge against inflation. When you own an apartment building the value and net income increases as the cost of plumbing, lumber and labor increases. And even more important—there are those who, like me, discover this exciting second career after retirement. Don't retire with no meaning to your remaining years, nothing to look forward to, nothing to get excited about. Just stop working at the old job and use some of your lifetime savings to put you in a new career. This may cause you to have problems, aggravations, and worries, such as a thinking human being should have—but you will be an active, contributing member of society, you will enjoy solving the problems, eliminating the aggravations, and replacing the worries with accomplishments.

A person of any age might consider ownership of an apartment building as a long or short term investment, devoting little time with little involvement in its operation. But, if you are retired or are soon-to-be-retired, you should consider it both as a long term investment and a new career; for you have the time to be involved and this book will give direction and purpose to your involvement.

And for the majority who must some day worry about retirement on a nominal company pension with the need for additional income—plan to apply for your Social Security retirement benefits at 65. Don't wait until age 72 merely because you need to supplement your pension. ($200 tax-free Social Security income is at least equal to $250 taxable earnings.) Need more? Go into business for yourself. The earnings from the Apartment Business is investment income and has no effect whatever on your right to collect Social Security retirement benefits at 65—or better yet—at 62.

For the retired executive accustomed to running the show and making decisions, the ownership/operation of an apartment building can be the fulfillment of his lifetime career—now he can be the sole 100% stockholder with no Board of Directors to appease. He will make a marvelous landlord for he is accustomed to spending money to maintain equipment and property.

But no matter what your age and circumstance, if you are seeking a second career, an opportunity for profits dependent to a large extent upon your ingenuity as an "operator," consider becoming the owner of one or more apartment buildings. And if you are a landlord now, please read the pages that follow with an open mind. If you do that, I can virtually guarantee that this book will increase your profits and your satisfaction substantially.

Chapter II

PROPER OPERATION

or

how to or who says

Before I proceed to tell you *how to*, you have the right to know *who says*. So here are my credentials.

I had spent 40 years in the life insurance business and was considered successful in every phase of the industry. Beginning as a salesman I progressed to manager, vice president, president, chairman of the board of a life insurance company and I retired to accept occasional assignments as a consultant to insurance companies. I seemed to have an affinity for property. I fell in love with a building just as some people fall in love with a piece of art. It didn't matter if it was a run-down shack, a mansion, vacant land or an office building, I fell in love with all types. So I bought property, both

5

as an individual investment and also for company invest-
ments. To date, I have purchased a total of four single homes,
four apartment buildings, and five commercial buildings.
These properties range from $18,000 to $1,250,000.

During the last seven years of my insurance career I was an
absentee owner of a 14 unit apartment building. I was certain
I was operating it in a business-like fashion, but I have since
discovered that that was not so. I did not enjoy it. It was only a
tax shelter and an annual out-of-pocket loss—so I sold it for
the same amount that I had paid seven years earlier. Then I
had to pay the tax on my "profit" (depreciation taken over the
previous seven years).

However, when I retired from my full-time occupation, no
one was surprised that I began to invest in property to keep me
from the boredom and feeling of uselessness of retirement.
But I had another purpose—to increase my fixed income and
ride the wave of inflation. During the past few years I have
been paying attention to and operating apartments as a
business and I am enjoying it. In fact, I am not retired. I am so
busy I don't know how I ever had time for work. I recently
refused the presidency of a life insurance company because I
get much more satisfaction out of the apartment business.

At the present time I am the owner of three apartment
buildings. One is composed of seven apartments, six
2-bedroom and one 3-bedroom; the second is an eight unit
building with six 1-bedroom and two 2-bedroom apartments;
and the third is 13 units with a mixture of five 3's, five 2's, two
1's and one bachelor. This gives me a total of 28 units, all
unfurnished, and makes me an expert. All three buildings are
within a radius of three miles and I expect to add a fourth and
maybe a fifth building within the same area.

The application of my insurance experience to the operation
of apartments is producing unusual results. The life insurance

business is built on developing a clientele, keeping in touch with and servicing the same clientele, and maintaining that clientele. A life insurance salesman knows it is more profitable to do business with his present customers than to ignore them and concentrate on the search for new customers. He keeps in touch with his clientele by sending letters occasionally, mailing birthday cards regularly, and making a personal call at least once a year.

The apartment building owner, however, seems to be ruled by a strange philosophy. He also must develop a "clientele" of tenants but he is told not to co-mingle—stay aloof from tenants. Do not cater to present tenants because constant turnover is "the name of game." Therefore, there is little effort made nor any interest shown in satisfying the old tenants. Many apartment house managers are also under the delusion that their only important function is to secure new tenants, and they take pride in being called "a good renter." What a waste! The owners and managers who accept constant turnover as a way of apartment life have no conception whatever of proper operation or the potential of their income property.

Collecting rents is not all there is to owning apartments— you must really love your building and appreciate your tenants—otherwise get out of this business.

Chapter III

THE TYPICAL OWNER

or

some do and some can't

I have no business criticizing a man who purchases a building and neglects it—or even wrecks it. He owns it and he has the right to do whatever he wishes with his property.

But, virtually no owner *intends* to neglect or wreck his property—it just happens to work out that way—maybe because of a misconception that ownership/operation of apartment buildings is just a static investment. Instead, it is the most active business investment you can make. But I believe I know why it happens to buildings owned by certain types of owners.

The typical apartment building owner seems to fit into one of three major groups.

Group I is composed of the far-removed, disinterested, aloof absentee owner. This owner made an investment with the assurance that it would require no personal involvement whatsoever. He is the real estate man's pigeon. He owns a building that was selected for him by his real estate man—and sells and buys again when the realtor and accountant decide he should do so. He would not live in the building himself and he never visits the place. He takes no pride of ownership in the building but leaves all operations to the manager and/or his realtor. The manager's only incentive is to fill up the building so that he will not have to be confined there on the weekends. This is a very cold impersonal situation where the only authority the manager has is to collect rents, and all requests for maintenance have to be referred to the "front office." If the manager happens to be considerate of his obligations he may, despite the absentee owner, operate the building efficiently and profitably. But this group of owners do not get the long term profits nor the satisfaction of owning an apartment house because they "get out" of their buildings for the same reason they "got in"—no good reason.

Group II is another large group. A professional investment company puts together a "syndicate" of a number of individuals who collectively own one large building of from 50 to 100 or more units. This is even more cold and more impersonal. To most owners this was, is, and always will be nothing more than a tax shelter. However, to the company that put the deal together and sold it to the group, it is a constant source of profit. They cannot lose, for in addition to a commission or a fee for setting up the syndicate, they usually get 5% of the gross rental income for managing the building. The owners must also support a manager on the premises who gets 5% or more for on the job management. This manager has the same incentive—emphasis is on filling all vacancies as soon as possible—rather than preventing vacancies. And this manager really has to refer every request for expenditure to the "front office"—and *each year* he has to deliver notices of increases in rent decided upon by the "front office" despite the fact that he has six vacancies and the increases will create more vacancies.

Group III, the largest group, is composed of people who individually own an apartment building usually, from four to as many as 20 or 30 units. This owner selected his own building carefully. He has a large part of his assets invested in that building. He usually lives there and manages the building himself. He has a far different incentive from the previous non-owner managers. He wants to have only long term tenants. Therefore, he must qualify them. The apartment that has just been recarpeted, repainted, sparkling clean, must now be rented to someone who must stay two or three years in order to amortize this big expense. So the owner will not rent to a man who offers the full rent plus deposits in *cash* and who wishes to move in today. We have all met such a prospective tenant. In fact, it always occurs on a Saturday or Sunday when you cannot check him—and sometimes (as I know from personal experience) he even happens to have all his furniture on a U-Haul truck at the curb.

At the beginning of this chapter I referred to neglecting and wrecking buildings. Who does this? Mainly owners in Groups I and II—and I repeat, never on purpose; it just happens that way. The Group I owner, being disinterested in the long term aspects of his investment, will tend to "take the cream off the top"—that is, collect rents but neglect repairs and cosmetic improvements. A few years later he sells a neglected run-down building. Inflation of property values often enables him to at least get the price he paid, even though it is a run-down building. But this owner did not enhance the landlord image to the tenants that passed through his building.

As for Group II—it is purely and simply a matter of paying out no more than you take in. And when the "take in" is not sufficient, this building of 100 or more units starts to deteriorate—but fast. The first sign of decay cannot be seen because it is always behind locked doors—it is called "cannibalism." This means that when Apartment #42 must be recarpeted, he takes the carpeting out of vacant Apartment #43. And soon a broken dining room light fixture means that another vacant apartment is stripped of its light fixture. And when it gets down to toilet seats—watch out! Then the 20 owners are asked to kick in some more money—and some want out right away.

Just to set the record straight, I am not condemning all syndicated buildings. Many are efficiently operated and make good on their projections to their investors. But more than a few have been in trouble and still more will be in financial difficulties. And so-called big names, both of the promoting organization and/or individual investors, have not been immune from catastrophic results. Obviously those most vulnerable are the owners who have paid far more than the true value of the building and where the tenant occupancy has never reached the point where the rental income is sufficient to meet the expenses.

So an "in-trouble" building in this group also creates more anti-landlord sentiment for the tenants keep getting less of the services they were promised. And there are plenty of consumer or legal aid groups that would show the tenants how to organize a tenants' strike.

Group III will also have a few owners who neglect their buildings, but this will be due to ignorance or greed. The ignorant I can take care of—all they need is a copy of this book. The greedy I can't help, because they wouldn't spend any money for a book that preaches enlightened self-interest, which may mean deferring immediate profits for long range opportunities, and—to coin a phrase—spending money to make money.

I find it interesting that Groups I and II favor leases for one, two, or three years, whereas Group III tends to use month-to-month agreements. Yet (although I have no statistics to prove this—only my experience), I'll bet Group III has longer-term tenants.

I do have some statistics that prove that Group III is a very important factor in supplying the housing needs of our nation (according to the Census Bureau 1971 Survey of Residential Finance). There are 7,000,000 small rental properties (1, 2, 3 and 4 units) in the United States, of which 6,200,000 are owned by individual owners. Medium-sized properties (5 to 49 units) total approximately 500,000, of which over 75% are owned by individual owners.

Another interesting discovery of the survey: The larger properties (over 50 units) charge higher rents than the smaller properties in relation to the value of the property. To the investor in the larger properties this means the projection of a better return on his investment because of higher rentals in proportion to the value of the larger property compared to the smaller property. Therefore, many investors follow the experts' advice (and projections of the higher rentals) and they invest in the larger buildings.

However, I also interpret this to mean that the tenant can get a comparable apartment for a lower rental in a smaller building. So I say—if the tenant gets a better buy in the smaller building (and your projections based on lower rentals give you a satisfactory return), better follow my advice and buy a smaller building.

Chapter IV

HOW LARGE A BUILDING

or

think small

How large a building should you purchase?

Assume that this is your first income property venture.

I do not care whether you have $15,000 or $150,000 to invest—my answer would be the same—buy from 8 to 10 to 15 units—unfurnished—never, *never*, consider furnished apartments.

Let's dispose of this question of furnished or unfurnished apartments right now. This book espouses the cause of apartment buildings as a sound investment, even for a novice investor who can only work at it part-time and who does not wish to be completely immersed with this one investment. If the apartments are furnished, you must become totally involved and must have a strong back for you will be forever moving furniture and forever re-renting. You will never be able to relax with the feeling that all your apartments are rented with no vacancy in the immediate future. Furnished apartments do have a place—no-bedroom apartments, called singles or bachelors, are always furnished and so they should be—for whoever heard of requiring an overnight hotel guest to bring his own furniture.

My advice to you is, don't even look at a building that has furnished apartments—unless they are all one or two bedroom and the price is right—so that you can throw out the furniture and convert it to an unfurnished building. So I repeat, 8 to 15 units (doesn't matter one, two or three bedrooms) for your first venture, also for your second, also for your third, etc.

The experts will not agree with me. Tell your banker, your mortgage loan man, your accountant, your doctor, your lawyer—tell anyone of them that you are planning to buy two or three small apartment buildings—and in every instance they will advise that you invest instead in *one* large building. The doctor or lawyer won't know why—but they heard that advice somewhere. The banker, mortgage loan man, accountant—they will know why. The why is "you will have much less expense since you will need only one manager and you will only have to repair one roof, one swimming pool. With three small buildings, you will have three managers, three roofs, three swimming pools."

These arguments are almost wholly fallacious. First, the costs for three managers is, if anything, less than the cost for one manager of a large building—and the three are usually better managers than the one "good" one because they have much less managing to do. Second, the cost of re-roofing is about the same for 30 units at one location or 30 units at three locations. Third, there is no doubt that the expense for three swimming pools is three times as much as one pool, but I recommend *no* pools—and smaller buildings are amenable to no pools, whereas the larger buildings are not.

So I tell you the "experts" are wrong. And I believe you will agree by the time you finish this book.

Chapter V

HOW TO LOOK FOR A BUILDING

or

search

Most people expect real estate agents to be experts, and most knowledgeable as to property values. I find their expertise, especially in property values, to be grossly over-rated. They may be expert salesmen but don't look to them for advice as to whether or not any particular building is for you—you and you alone must make that final determination. (That's what this book is all about.) And don't expect the real estate man to instruct you on how to properly operate an apartment building—for this is outside the scope of selling. This involves the social obligation to the tenant which, if properly met, gives the owner the ultimate in satisfaction and the greatest return on his investment.

The real estate agent is naturally interested in selling the property but he usually knows very little about the building. Of course he has a few pertinent figures, such as gross income and gross expenses, but you will note at the bottom of every prospectus that he always disclaims any responsibility for the accuracy of those figures. He doesn't know the building for he has, in many instances, never even set foot in it. He doesn't know the condition of each apartment—the roof, the plumbing, the tenants—yet his advice to you is "Buy the building." It is most uncommon to find a real estate agent who will tell you not to buy one of his buildings—that it is over-priced or that it is a problem building. When you do find such a realtor, adopt him as your own for he can save you money and help you avoid serious errors.

Now that I have "tarred and feathered" real estate men as a whole let me tell you again: A qualified realtor is a good man to have on your side. I found an exceptionally fine realtor who was an expert in income property as he had many years of personal involvement as owner and operator. My experience with him was as outstandingly good as my experience with most others was outstandingly lousy. Let me prove it to you—the good, I mean. I met him when I walked into his office (the closest to my property) and asked him to list my property for sale. He knew every building in his area including mine and he asked why I wanted to sell. I told him that I was too busy to be bothered with the maintenance and rental problems. The tenants were pests and the maintenance a damn nuisance (did I say that?). When I left his office a few hours later my building was not for sale. He not only talked me out of selling but he gave me the use of his maintenance men (at cost) and his rental service (at no cost).

Two years later, I wanted to buy a business property which was listed by another realtor. Whom did I call? Right! I called my realtor and asked him to check it out. To my surprise he actually checked the property, whereas I only meant to check the price. It was for sale for $135,000 but someone had made a $120,000 offer which was pending. I authorized my friend to rush in with a $135,000 offer. He didn't. He told me later that if he had, the other buyer might have raised his offer to meet mine. He waited a whole week until the other offer was rejected and then he bought it for me for $130,000.

A few days later I asked him to check on the adjoining property. He advised me the owner would sell for $105,000. I authorized the purchase for $105,000 because I needed it to complete my parking requirements for the building I planned to construct. He told me "to keep my shirt on." He offered $95,000 and I bought it for $97,500.

A week later I asked him to check on the "across the street" abandoned gas station. (Corner of course—where else would a gas station be?) It was for sale for $84,000. I knew better than to offer $84,000 now. I just said "Buy it." To my surprise he didn't—and I didn't—because my realtor checked the property and found that the City had a 20 foot street easement (allowing them to widen the street by taking 20 feet away from the gas station lot), which meant the lot was not good for the purpose I had in mind.

So you see there are some good realtors too who earn their commission and teach you to check both the property and your offer.

Since real estate firms have the listings, you should look to them for a building. But do not depend on them entirely to the exclusion of all other sources. You can also purchase direct from the owner. However, this does not mean you are getting it for less money than through a commissioned agent. I have seen many cases where it would cost even more. So although you should check the newspaper ads for the "SALE BY OWNER," I also suggest that you compare them to the real estate man's listings.

As a rule, view all listings as being over-priced. Check the asking price against the gross rental income and net rental income (defined in Chapters 7 and 8), but because of my "pride of ownership" requirement, you will find that most of them are not for you at any price.

Despite some notable exceptions, I have met too many realtors who have no business in income property, for they have little knowledge about the property beyond the price. I have found not only ignorant real estate men, but even owners who didn't know how many two bedroom apartments were in the building they were trying to sell to me. I have had to come to the conclusion that many real estate men will accept a listing from an owner at any price in order to get the listing.

Still, the best way to start to look for a building is to talk to real estate people and check their ads carefully. If you have a realtor that you know and one that you prefer to do business with, let him follow through on any other realtor's ads, for they usually cooperate or are in multiple listing. Your realtor can save you a lot of leg work. If you are talking to a new-to-you realtor, ask him for the address of the advertised listing that interested you enough to make this inquiry. Do not go to see the building with the real estate man. Insist that he give you the address so that you might see the exterior of the building. Otherwise you are going to waste much time going with real estate men to buildings that you do not care for because you immediately dislike the exterior, or its locality. You are going to have trouble at first with many a realtor who will refuse to give you addresses of buildings. He will insist that he must go with you to the building before he can give you its address. This is pure poppycock. Tell him to give you a list of addresses and that you will write your name on that list, so that should you purchase any of those buildings, he will be entitled to claim a commission. With that assurance on your part, no legitimate real estate man should refuse to give you the addresses.

The last building I purchased was the result of my looking at 63 different buildings—that is 63 exteriors—but I only got into five buildings. In other words, I eliminated 58 buildings because I did not care for the exterior or the locality of the building. What a waste of time it would have been had I met the real estate man in his office (as he insisted in every case) and I had him drive me to 63 buildings. Then there is an additional waste of time, for he will often insist that you go inside because he made an appointment with a manager or owner to show you the building.

Note: For research purposes for this book, I deserted my realtor and went directly to each realtor who had the listing.

You never get to see all the apartments and yet you are expected to, and you do, make offers and give deposits on the building. Usually the excuse is that the seller does not wish to have his tenants know the building is for sale, so all you get to see is the manager's apartment and one or two vacant apartments out of a 12 unit building. Don't worry. Make certain your offer is subject to your seeing (and approving in writing) all apartments—that gives you an *out* after you get *in*.

I gave deposits (one at one time) and made offers on four of the five buildings that I had partially checked interior-wise.

The first offer was not accepted. They stood firm on their asking price which was much too high.

The second offer (on twin 9 unit buildings) was accepted—so I then checked all 18 apartments and they were immaculately maintained. However, I noted that the carports were empty except for two VW's—at night. Before I make an offer I always check a building at night after dark, and I do that for two or three nights in a row *after* I have made a deposit on a building. I was puzzled. Never were there more than two VW's in the carports. So I decided to try to park my medium-sized car in a carport and found it was very difficult to get in, and almost impossible to get out. So, I withdrew my offer.

The third offer was accepted, but the apartments I had not seen previously were disastrous. My offer was much too high for the condition of this building—so I withdrew it.

My fourth offer was accepted so I checked the apartments. They were as I expected—some worse, some better, so I ended up purchasing number four.

This took a lot of time and, though I had made deposits on the other three, it would have been a serious error if I had purchased any one of them, even though they did qualify from an exterior and a locality standpoint.

Chapter VI

HOW TO LOOK AT A BUILDING

or

research

In order for you to really be able to check a building you must have a form listing all pertinent physical features.

It must be comprehensive in order to compare a number of buildings so that you might eliminate and reduce the list to a few—then you have a good chance of making a correct decision. Don't trust to memory; write it down immediately. Don't use the back of an envelope, use a form such as my "Look-at Check List" on the following page. Without such a form I don't know how you can come to any kind of a sensible conclusion.

25

Form A-20

PART 1 – 'LOOK-AT' CHECK LIST –

NAME OF BUILDING AND/OR ADDRESS   REAL ESTATE AGENT   PHONE   AGE OF BUILDING

CITY   OWNER'S NAME   PHONE   NO. OF UNITS

EXTERIOR: Style—Composition—Windows

LOCATION: Very Good—Good—O.K.—No Good:

POOL: HEATED: CONDITION: POOL DECK AREA:

No. OF 3 BEDROOM	2 BED	1 BED	SINGLES	NO. STALL SHOWERS

No. BATHROOMS IN 3'S   No. IN 2'S   CONDITION OF BATHROOMS (Windows or Exhaust Fans); Heaters)

BUILT-INS: REFRIGERATORS: DRAPES AND CONDITION:

TYPE AND MAKE OF HEATING SYSTEM: CARPETING—QUALITY—COLOR—CONDITION:

1ST FLOOR: SLAB—PLYWOOD—HARDWOOD   2ND FLOOR: ELASTIZEL—PLYWOOD—HARDWOOD (SQUEEKY?)

WALLS: LATHE & PLASTER—WALL BOARD   PRIVATE PATIOS: CEILINGS: WATER STAINS-PAINT

SECURITY: TYPE OF ROOF: CONDITION:

OUTSIDE STAIRS: MAGNESITE—STEEL   OPEN DECK & LANDINGS: MAGNESITE—   CONDITION:

A/C MAKE: SIZE: CONDITION: DRIP ON DECK:

EXTERIOR PAINT: TRIM: DOORS:

PEEPHOLES:

DOOR BELLS:

CONDITION MAIL BOXES:

SCREEN DOORS:

WINDOW SCREENS:

NO. OF CARPORTS:

GARAGES:

OPEN SPACES:

SIZE—SPACES ADEQUATE—TIGHT:

STORAGE LOCKERS FOR TENANTS:

DRIVEWAY AND EGRESS—VERY GOOD—GOOD—ADEQUATE—TIGHT—IMPOSSIBLE:

LAUNDRY ROOM SIZE:

NO. OF WASHERS—DRYERS:

OWNED OR LEASED:

LAUNDRY LOCKERS FOR TENANTS:

LAUNDRY AVERAGE MONTHLY INCOME:

STORAGE FOR BUILDING SUPPLIES / EQUIPMENT:

SIZE OF ROOMS AS TO LARGE — O.K. — SMALL — TOO SMALL:

KITCHENS _____ BEDROOMS: _____ WINDOWS _____

LIVING ROOM:

DINING AREA:

GUEST CLOSET IN L/R

SIZE OF CLOSETS IN BEDROOMS — SLIDING DOORS? — CLOSETS CARPETED — LIGHTED?

ANY UNITS FURNISHED:

FURNITURE CONDITION:

FURNITURE OWNED OR LEASED:

HOT WATER SUPPLIED BY:

CONDITION H/W HEATERS:

ADEQUATE HOT WATER:

OUTDOOR SITTING SPACE:

BARBECUE:

CHAIRS—TABLES—STATUARY, ETC., ITEMIZE TO CONVEY:

SPRINKLERS:

OUTDOOR SPOTLITES AND BUILDING ILLUMINATION:

LOT SIZE:

INTERIOR PAINT CONDITION: (How many apartments seen?)

ADULTS:

CHILDREN:

PETS:

LEASES:

MONTH-TO-MONTH:

CLEANING DEPOSITS:

SECURITY DEPOSITS:

KEY DEPOSITS:

HOW CLOSE TO FOOD MARKET:

PUBLIC TRANSPORTATION:

SCHOOLS:

FREEWAY:

PART 2 – "LOOK-AT" CHECK LIST

ARE ARCHITECT'S PLANS AVAILABLE (IF INTERESTED IN BUYING, STUDY THEM BEFORE OFFER):

TERMITE SERVICE:	PEST CONTROL SERVICE:	ANY OTHER REGULAR SERVICE:

WHAT KIND OF STRUCTURE IS THERE ON ALL FOUR SIDES?

EAST: WEST:

NORTH: SOUTH:

WOULD I LIVE HERE? COULD I LIVE HERE? DATE:

PRESENT SCHEDULED INCOME:

	Occupied Since	No. of Bed.	Mthly Rent
Apt. 1.			$
2.			
3.			
4.			
5.			
6.			
7.			
8.			

	Occupied Since	No. of Bed.	Mthly Rent
9.			$
10.			
11.			
12.			
13.			
14.			
15.			
16.			

TOTAL SCHEDULED ANNUAL INCOME . . . . $

PRESENT ANNUAL EXPENSES

Real Estate Taxes . . . . . . $ _____

Insurance . . . . _____

Utilities . . . . _____

Manager . . . . _____

Gardener . . . . _____

Rubbish . . . . _____

Pool . . . . _____

Maintenance . . . . _____   5% of Annual Income

Vacancy . . . . _____   5% of Annual Income

Miscellaneous . . . . _____

TOTAL . . . . $ _____

Present 1st Mortgage
Amount $ _____   Monthly Payment $ _____   Int. Rate: _____ %   No. Yrs. to go: _____

Is it Assumable: _____   Mortgagor: _____

2nd Mortgage: $ _____   Details: _____

ASKING PRICE: $ _____   ÷ $ _____   =   Price on 'Times Earnings' Basis

                              Gross Annual Income

I was seriously considering becoming a real estate salesman upon retirement. But my "Look-at Check List" produced so many negative items about most buildings that I realized I could not possibly sell income property. My experience proved that I had to study at least 15 buildings in order to find one worth considering. If I were in the real estate business that would mean I would have to look at 15 properties before I could accept one listing, and that is no way to succeed as a real estate salesman.

Don't complete the "Look-at" details until you have approved the exterior and location. The only way that I can help you to qualify the exterior or location of a building is to put you through the truth test. Answer this question truthfully: "Would *you* live in such a building and/or such a location?" If you would not live in a building that looked like the building you are looking at—if you would not live in that location— turn it down. My feeling is that you must purchase "pride of ownership" buildings. This does not mean that it has to look like the Taj Mahal, or be an imposing edifice. It could even be in a so-called slum area. But it should make you feel good owning it, not ashamed. It doesn't matter whether the rentals are $75.00 or $400.00 per, never, never buy a building of which you would not freely admit ownership.

You do not necessarily have to live in that building. Continue to live in your $100,000 home, but buy a building where, although the rentals are most nominal in comparison to your present living standard, should you have business reverses, should your children grow up and leave you, should your house burn down, if you had to live there yourself, you could do so without being ashamed of the address. (Business reversals might, for example, make such a move necessary.)

And pride of ownership is especially essential for the retired owner. He should seriously consider living in his own building, thereby getting a permanent tenant and cutting his living costs, which in turn increases his fixed income. Since he would also be living where he works, he would be cutting his gasoline expense. The retired owner can thus retire to his place of business—and if it is good enough for the owner, I am sure it will attract his type of tenant customers.

I would be happy to live in any one of my three buildings. In fact, I do now live in one of my buildings and find it to be most satisfying—again. breaking the experts rule that the owner should never live in his apartment building.

Your first look at a building requires only the address and the real estate agent's name. Drive out and see the exterior. Most of your checklist forms will contain addresses and nothing more. You will reject most of the buildings and save considerable time. I doubt that you can find a building where you do *not* like the exterior and location which still merits going in to check the interior. A favorable interior cannot overcome an unfavorable exterior and locality. Prospective tenants do not look at the interior if they have rejected the exterior—and neither should a prospective buyer.

When I refer to exterior, I do not mean that you should reject the building because it needs a paint job. I do not mean that you should turn it down because the window screens are broken or because the place looks like a fixer-upper. A neglected or fixer-upper building is often the best buy of all and gives the new owner the fun and satisfaction of restoring a building for an appreciative group of present tenants and the entire neighborhood.

Chapter VII

HOW MUCH TO PAY

or

make like you know

Apartment houses that are for sale are usually five or ten years old or older. They are not new. If they are, don't buy them—buy a five or ten year old building. The reason five years is a popular selling point is that the newness has worn off. When a vacancy occurs now it requires a complete redecorating job including new carpets, new drapes, etc. Maintenance begins to be a constant problem to an absentee owner. So the buyer should be aware of this additional expense when he is bidding for a building.

If the building is ten years old there is usually less redecorating expense than for the five year old. All of the ten year apartments have their "second set of teeth"—that is, the original carpeting and drapes have been replaced and some only within the last year or two, whereas in a five year old building none of them may have been replaced. There is, however, a bit more maintenance for the ten year buyer, for this is the time the garbage disposal might have to be replaced. But this is not a major item; not to a new owner who expects it. It is a major nuisance to the present owner for he isn't accustomed to this type of expense.

There are, however, two major expense items facing the new owner of a ten year old building which he should take into consideration. The exterior of the building needs a paint job and the roof is about due or overdue for a re-roofing job. Both of these are capital improvements. They improve the property and will attract new tenants. They will also increase present tenants pride in their home and make your investment more profitable. So the buyer should be aware of this expense but he should also be prepared to make these improvements immediately (paint immediately, re-roof as soon as leaks develop) otherwise his investment is off to a bad start.

Between six to seven times gross rental income is a simple guideline for establishing the price you should pay, but first let's make certain we understand rental income. Do not accept rental figures given by the seller without checking—especially as to vacant apartments. The seller knows the "six to seven" formula so it behooves him to show a higher rental. My experience, however, has been that these figures are almost always given correctly—but watch out for the exception.

Your offer is based on *gross* rental income. Gross rental income obviously is the total income of the building *prior* to any expenses. If you are looking at a 10 unit building renting for $100 a month each, the annual gross rental income is $1,200 x 10 = $12,000. I would not hesitate to offer six times $12,000 or $72,000, even though it was a five or ten year old building as described above, which would require immediate maintenance.

I would be glad to pay seven times $12,000 or $84,000 if the seller was an owner/operator as recommended by this book, for then the exterior has been painted recently, the roof is a new one, the apartments all have near new carpeting, the tenants are happy. Therefore, I am inheriting a "full house."

And to prove that I am inconsistent, I would even pay as much as eight times gross if the exterior, location, maintenance, and tenancy were above par and the rental schedule was way below par.

Although the gross rental income shown by the seller is most often a true figure, there are exceptions that cause you to put it to the "smell test." I recall an 8 unit building that had a beautiful exterior and a superb location. The owner lived on the premises and he set an unrealistically high rent on his own apartment which obviously increased the gross rental income. I was suspicious so I asked to look at the rental leases early in the negotiations. They were all over two years old—some four and five—but they had either expired and were continuing on a month-to-month basis, or were about to expire. This co-incidence made me doubly suspicious so I unobtrusively jotted down the name and business address of one of the tenants. I called on him and told him I was about to purchase the building and that I could not afford to make a bad invest-ment, therefore, I was doing some checking. I told him that I would guarantee not to raise his rent for at least two years if he would answer a few questions—and I added, I would not raise his rent even if he did not answer any questions. I asked whether he planned to renew his soon-to-expire three year lease and found that he had only lived there three months; he was paying no rent whatever since the seller owed him a substantial amount of money. He was furious to learn that the property he had just moved to was up for sale, so he added the information that the owner had three apartments tenanted by members of his family. What a set-up this expert (meaning me) almost walked into, fake leases and at least four out of eight apartments owner-occupied, and at unrealistically high fake rentals. And the seller seemed to be such a nice guy. His ad said: "Buy direct from owner—no real estate commission." No decent real estate man, if he knew the facts, would have touched this listing.

There's another exception for you to watch out for, especially in Southern California. Whenever a building has a bachelor apartment, meaning one room which is both the living room and bedroom (plus a bathroom) BUT NO KITCHEN, make sure you look at the walls of that one room. Look for a camouflaged door. Make certain it is not the third bedroom and the second bathroom from the adjoining now castrated two bedroom and one bath apartment. Another way to check on the bachelor apartments: go outside and count the gas and electric meters. If there are eleven apartments of which two are listed as bachelors but there are only nine gas meters, then there are only nine apartments, for the bachelors are illegal and in violation of the building code. They were split off from adjoining apartments in order to increase the rental income. In this case, there was a real estate man who had this listing and whose prospectus stated clearly "eleven apartments."

So back to my guide lines: Six times gross rental income is what I would pay for the building with average or even more than average maintenance required and with average or even below average long term tenancy.

I would pay up to seven times gross for the well maintained building with good stable tenants. (Ultra exceptional—up to eight.)

I would also not hesitate to pay 4½ to 5½ times an assumed gross rental for a neglected, partially unoccupied (or occupied by neglectful tenants) building in a distressed or so-called slum area—provided that I would, if I had to, live in the building myself and accept the social obligation of improving it, thus helping to upgrade the slum area, eliminate the eye sore—and make a lot of money too.

Chapter VIII

WHICH ONE TO BUY

or

eeney, meeney, miney, whoa

All of my assumptions are based on a cash down payment of 25% of the purchase price leaving a first mortgage of 75% but no second or third mortgages. In addition you will need money for closing costs, maintenance or rehabilitation. Figure a minimum of another 5% of the purchase price. Therefore, do not go into income property unless you have at least 30 or 35% of the purchase price available for the investment.

Do not buy any property unless you can expect an annual cash flow return of 10% of the money that you invested. Cash flow means money in your pocket after all expenses, including the mortgage, monthly payments of interest *and principal*. Note: The amount of the principal payment is also profit, but it is not in your pocket. Depreciation is not profit, it merely defers income tax payments from this year to the year when you sell.

In order to establish a cash flow projection you must make assumptions of the cost of operation on a realistic basis. The assumed expenses of the building must be adequate, otherwise your projection is useless. You can usually accept the sellers' figures of expenses as valid as most sellers are honest. But you will find that their figures are often incomplete. They might be excused for not showing an annual expense for maintenance or a loss in rent income due to vacancies. But a real estate agent cannot be excused for such omissions. If the agent you are talking to does not refer to a vacancy percent factor and a maintenance percent factor as annual expense items, get yourself another agent.

Many buyers will assume 10% of gross rental income as an annual maintenance cost and also 10% as the vacancy factor. And in a badly operated building that will not be out of line. But after you buy and you spend the money immediately for necessary maintenance, you should, starting the second year, find that 5% for maintenance and 5% for vacancy is sufficient. I therefore use 5% in all of my projections because I am conceited enough to believe I can operate a building properly.

I must re-emphasize that my purpose is not tax shelter but enough cash flow to justify a 25% down payment. The "tax shelter investor" instead usually prefers a 10% to 15% down payment with a 2nd and sometimes even a 3rd mortgage— with almost no possibility of any cash flow.

To determine which building to buy, I do not revert to "eeney, meeney." I make a detailed comparison on a form that was not available, so I had to devise my own Comparative Work-Sheet (Form A-22).

Before I let you peek at the Comparative Work-Sheet, please turn back to Page 29. You will note that Present Annual Expenses (as reported by the seller) are listed. These are the operating expenses to be transferred to Form A-22. There is very little I can do to reduce taxes, insurance, utilities, etc. In fact, I expect such operating expenses to increase each year due to the ever-present inflation.

However, the Total Scheduled Annual Income (which is the present rent schedule) shown on Page 29—this figure I can do much about. Rents must increase due to inflation, but more important due to my upgrading the property.

So don't turn down a building you like merely because my Form A-22 produces a 7% cash flow. Many have low rent schedules that have not kept up with the times, just as the building has not been kept up. If there is a good probability of getting it up to a 10% cash flow in the near future—buy it.

Following is one of my completed Comparative Work-Sheets. You will see various mortgage interest rates, for although my study was over a period of only a few months—as time went by—interest rates went up.*

I purchased one of the five buildings shown on the following page but I should have purchased two. See if you can figure out which one I bought and which one I missed buying by just an hour.

---

*My last purchase entailed a mortgage at 8¾%. My next purchase will no doubt be at an even higher interest rate.

The rate of interest is material—but if the property will give me a fair cash flow on my investment—I guess I'll just have to pay the going rate.

COMPARATIVE WORK-SHEET

BUILDING ADDRESS:	111 Alpha St	222 Beta St	333 Chi St	444 Delta St	555 Epsilon Ave
AGE	10 YRS	10 YRS	18 YRS.	10 YRS	11 YRS.
ASKING PRICE	$117,000	$215,000	$65,000.	$83,000.	$170,000.
1. No. of Units	9	14	8	10	17
2. No. of 3's	—	13	—	—	—
3. " " 2's	9	—	2	3	10
4. " " 1's	—	1	6	6	*7
				1 SINGLE (LEGIT)	*3 FURNISHED
5. Parking	9 CARPORTS	15 CARPORTS	8 CARPORTS	9 CARPORTS	12 CARPORTS 5 OPEN SPACES
6. Rental 3's	—	$200 TO 225	—	—	—
7. " 2's	$165.	—	$120. & $130.	$145.	1 BATH $135. 1½ BATH $150.
8. " 1's	—	$135.	$90. To $105.	$115. ($90. SINGLE)	UNFURN. 120. FURN. 135.
9. Condition of Bldg.	GOOD EXC. PAINT	NEED PAINT & ROOF	EXCELLENT AND HAS NEW ROOF	GOOD	GOOD
10. Amt. for Rehab.	$1000.	$4000.	$300.	$500.	$300.
11. Offering Price	$110,000.	$200,000.	$63,000.	$83,000.	$170,000.
12. Amt. of Loan (75%)	$82,500.	150,000.	$45,000 7% ASSUMABLE 17 YEARS TO GO	62,250.	127,500.
13. Int. of Loan (25 yrs.)	8½%	8¼%		7¾%	8%

		INC. LAUNDRY				INC. OWNED LAUNDRY
14.	Yr. Gross Income	$18,000.	$33,540.	$10,380.	$14,580.	$27,120.
deduct 15.	Oper. Expense	7,334.	15,587.	4,711.	6,304.	10,547.
deduct 16.	Mtg. Loan Payt's	7,972.	14,193.	4,468.	5,666.	11,809.
equals Net Spendable or 17.	Cash Flow	2,694.	3,760.	1,201.	2,610.	4,764.
18.	Down Pay't (25%)	$27,500.	$50,000.	$18,000.	$20,750.	$42,500.
add 19.	Rehab. (Est.)	1,000.	4,000.	300.	500.	300.
add 20.	Assume 1½ points to obtain loan	1,238.	2,250.	—	623.	1,913.
add 21.	Escrow Fee plus Closing Costs (Est.)	135. / 250.	205 / 350	100. / 200.	105. / 200.	60. / 300.
equals 22.	Total Investment	$30,123.	$56,805.	$18,600.	$22,178.	$45,193.
23.	Cash Flow (same as 17)	$2,694.	$3,760.	$1,201.	$2,610.	$4,764.
24.	Cash Flow % of Total Investment	8.94%	6.61%	6.46%	11.76%	10.54%
25.	Price is how many times Yr. Gross Income	6.11	5.96	5.8	5.69	6.26
26.	Rent Schedule Evaluation	Maximum	Maximum	Much Too Low	Maximum due to Traffic Noise	Low
27.	Location Evaluation Up to 100% Outstanding	80%	80%	90%	70%	75%
		Next to Elem. School—Good for Family Rentals			Too Close to Freeway Noise	Stores+ Parking Lots at Rear—Good for Close-In Rentals

NOTE TO READER: Most of these figures come from Part 2 of Form A-20 'Look-At' Check List.

Chapter IX

THE APARTMENT HOUSE ASSOCIATION

or

dues, do's and don'ts

You have invested, or are thinking of investing, money in a business—and a business must maintain records of all its transactions. Membership in your local apartment house association will be most helpful. Even if you are not a joiner of organizations as a rule, you had better join this one. The forms available through an apartment association are absolutely essential for the novice, and valuable even for the experienced owner. Dues will be returned to you tenfold in many ways.

At a cost of only a few dollars you can obtain samples of all their forms, such as leases, applications to rent, receipts, overdue notices, eviction, etc. You can learn a great deal about your new business if you will study these forms. Through the association you can usually purchase a "Manual of Do's and Don'ts"—a landlord's manual—mainly DON'TS. This manual will help keep you out of legal entanglements, for you will soon discover that the law is pro-tenant and anti-landlord. In fact, you probably will be shocked to learn there is a book available in every book store telling tenants how to cheat the owner, how to live rent free, how to take advantage of pro-tenant legislation. So get your apartment house handbook on how to avoid being cheated.

The best insurance against being cheated is to use the association's "Application to Rent" form, and always use the credit investigative service offered through your apartment house association. This form is basic to proper management and it is so important it will be covered more fully in a chapter devoted to it exclusively.

You can frequently save time and money by making use of the services and goods advertised in your apartment house publications. The advertisers specialize in apartment services and know that the job has to be completed when promised because a tenant is about to move in.

I have found, in using these advertisers, that (with exceptions, of course) their prices are usually competitive and their service is better than you would generally get by selecting a painter or plumber at random out of the yellow pages. It makes good sense, if they are dependent on apartment business, that they are going to value the privilege of advertising in the apartment house association publication. And if one of them proves unreliable, you should report it to your association, as I recently had to do.

As an apartment house owner you are also entitled to discounts in many of the hardware and appliance stores. Do not hesitate to ask if they allow apartment house discounts. You will find this will save you a lot of money.

However, the most important function of the association is its awareness of pending legislation detrimental to the owner. By making its objections known to legislators, the association helps to block the passage of many more unfair, discriminatory anti-landlord laws than are already on the books.

The membership of apartment house associations is largely composed of owners of one or two small "pride of ownership" buildings. Their rentals represent an important part of their current income. To them, this is a serious business.

It is good business to join with them to protect your business.

Reprinted below, with permission, are some of the services offered by the Apartment Association of Los Angeles County, Inc. Other associations offer comparable services.

LOCAL ORDINANCES AND THE LAW – Our Association is active at local, state and national levels in protecting the rental industry against discriminatory laws. We present testimony on matters affecting you and your investment. We take court action where necessary. This activity is vital to your business and can only be successful with united owner action.

PRELIMINARY TENANT CHECKS – help owners avoid poor risk tenants and prevent costly trouble before it starts. This is the wise time to do it. We provide information almost immediately via telephone. A call to us is all it takes. This insurance pays off in advance. You cannot afford to be without it. Cost $3.50 for each report.

LEGAL FORMS – We carry current, updated legal forms designed to protect your dealings with tenants and the law. Use of these forms will help you avoid costly lawsuits and frustrating situations. They help you start right and prevent most bad endings. Members get 25% discount on orders of $2.00 or more. We can send forms by mail.

CONSULTING SERVICE – Whenever you have a problem, you can telephone our office at (213) 384-4131 and get help. In the 54 years this Association has been operating, we have learned many of the answers and owners get advice free. The value of this service is substantial.

MANAGER REFERRAL SERVICE – a tough problem these days, but we are able to help in many cases. We try to keep a list of available managers which we screen carefully. If you need a manager we *may* be able to help.

THE VACANCY PROBLEM – The heart of the rental business is full occupancy. We *try* to find you reliable tenants. We get calls these days from prospective tenants and work to improve this service in your interest.

MONTHLY MAGAZINE – Every member gets our monthly magazine in which we present a great deal of new information about the rental business. We summarize new products, new ideas, financial information, forecasts and trends in the rental business. The magazine. carries advertising from firms who supply products needed by the industry. These firms are screened for reliability so you can buy from them in confidence.

MEETINGS – We hold periodic meetings or seminars with round table discussions and qualified speakers who are experts in the rental industry. We advise dates and places.

OTHER SERVICES – We can suggest firms for discount buying; insurance, plumbing and electrical service, vending machine suppliers, books on apartment operation and other valuable services.

OFFICE STAFF – We have a full time paid office staff to service owners, however the Association is strictly non-profit with an elected Board of Directors. This Board meets monthly and serves without pay.

DUES – You will see from the dues schedule that it costs very little to belong. We operate economically and use every dollar for the benefit of the industry. We answer more than 100 inquiries every day using three telephones. Our job is to make sure when you join us, your dues are the best investment you could possibly make.

APARTMENT ASSOCIATION OF LOS ANGELES COUNTY, INC., 551 So. Oxford Street, Los Angeles, California 90020

Chapter X

OFFER, ESCROW, AND DEPOSIT

or

how to start before you begin

I start laying the proper foundation for my tenant relationship even before I am officially the new owner. But I cannot get to this "start" until I am in escrow. So please allow me to digress a bit and take a short-cut into escrow. I've been there many times so, better yet, I'll put you in escrow.

Note: If you live in a state where there are no escrow and/or title insurance companies, whenever I refer to escrow officer (or escrow) I refer you to your attorney.

You have decided on a building and are ready to make an

offer. If dealing with *your* realtor, he can help write the offer. If dealing with the *seller's* realtor, I suggest you go to your bank or savings and loan association and visit the escrow officer (or your attorney). Ask him to assist you in writing your offer correctly so that it is subject to termite clearance, conveyance of carpets, drapes, built-ins, inspection of all apartments and approval thereof in writing, time limit of acceptance of offer, etc.—and make your offer subject to escrow being opened at your bank.

The escrow officer cannot take the responsibility for the terms of your offer nor can he write it up for you, but he can be of great assistance by suggesting a word or two as long as it appears in your handwriting.

I feel better when the escrow department of my bank or savings and loan association is handling all the funds even though all escrow companies are neutral and represent both parties. You are the buyer. You are the most important part to this transaction. Without you, there is no transaction.

The printed offer form of the real estate firm usually says in small print that escrow should be opened in a certain escrow company. This is what I object to. Although you sign the realtor's printed form, make sure the offer is in your words (the words that have been checked by your bank or attorney) and cross out the reference to "their" escrow firm. Give the real estate man the deposit check made payable to your bank, rather than to the real estate firm. He will not object, for you have the right to have all your money, including the deposit, handled through escrow.

Your offer has been accepted and while awaiting the title search and the closing of the deal you do something that no expert, no real estate man ever heard of—you go visiting. Call on the manager of the building first. Tell him you are going to be the new owner. Tell him you are now going to call on every one of the tenants personally. Call on them and tell them that the seller is going to transfer to you all of the deposits that are to the credit of any tenant, therefore you would like to have them complete a Confirmation of Deposits Form. (See the following example.)

CONFIRMATION FORM

CONFIRMATION of Deposits / Rent / Furnishings as of _____ 197___.

Address _____ City/State _____

Zip _____

Apartment No. _____

Name _____

Family Members _____

_____

_____

Pets _____

Deposits

Key . . . . $ _____

Cleaning Fee . . . $ _____

Security/Damage . . $ _____

Last Month's Rent . $ _____

Rent

Monthly . . . . . $ _____

Now paid to . . . . $ _____

Payable each month on the _____ in advance

Furnishings owned by landlord

Carpeting _____   Drapes _____

Stove/Oven _____   Refrigerator _____

Dishwasher _____   Light Fixtures _____

Furniture _____   (If any, list on reverse of Form)

Any Rental Agreement in writing _____   Date of Agreement now in effect _____

Living here since _____

Garage Space No. _____   Locker No. _____

Type of Auto _____   Color _____   License Plate No. _____

Signed: _____

This confirmation form is to determine whether or not the person has any deposits, such as last month's rent or damage deposit or key deposit—deposits which are supposed to be turned over to you by the present owner. Many owners do not keep good records. In many instances, they do not know the amount of the deposits received from each tenant, especially if the tenant has been there one or two years. And don't be surprised to discover the tenant doesn't know either. Discrepancies must be resolved before it becomes your responsibility. Make the seller assume his obligation before you take over. This form also gives you an opportunity to check appliances such as refrigerators, drapes, hanging light fixtures, etc., that should be conveyed to you. These refrigerators and fixtures were included in establishing the rental charges for each apartment. Therefore, you are entitled to have transferred to you the ownership of these specific appliances.

This confirmation form has turned up many discrepancies and a few refrigerators. Especially check the drapes. A number of tenants have replaced the building drapes with their own and no one knows the whereabouts of the old drapes. The seller who has sold you a building as carpeted and draped, must make good for the missing drapes. The tenants, in every case, have been pleased to have their deposits confirmed by the new owner. I make certain to tell them that I am not yet the new owner and that they will be notified when it is official, so that the rent thereafter would be paid to me *in advance.*

My reference to *paying rent in advance* also brought forth a number of interesting comments. For example, I was told by more than one tenant that they do not pay their rent in advance. They are always a month behind. They were unhappy with my statement that I expected rent to be paid in advance. I discovered some tenants were as much as three months in arrears, a problem which the seller obviously was well aware of. The Confirmation Form thus gave me an opportunity to appraise the tenancy. Although I was already committed to purchase the property, I now knew in advance which tenants were going to be problem payers, and would have to be replaced.

A run-down, neglected building creates neglectful tenants. When a two bathroom apartment has only one functioning toilet for four months, I cannot blame the tenant for being in arrears. I had two tenants tell me upon my taking over one of my buildings that they would be moving within a month or two. But when I gave prompt attention to all neglected maintenance (including repairing the toilet), repainting the exterior of the building, landscaping, roofing, new patio, cleaning up the premises—both tenants who stated that they were going to move changed their mind and the tenants who were in arrears became prompt up-to-date payers. So I maintain that a building that is maintained will create for you a tenancy that will also be maintained.

I do not stop with the Confirmation Form, for as soon as the escrow is closed, I mail a letter to the same tenants telling them that I take pride in ownership and I expect the tenants to take pride in their own apartment. A copy of the letter that I have used follows:

April 25, 19XX

TO ALL TENANTS - XXX FANCY AVE.

This is to advise you that the ownership of this building has been transferred effective May 1st, 19XX.

We are *very* pleased to be the new owners. We purchased this building because it is an unusually well constructed attractive structure -- with tenants who obviously thought likewise since they chose this as their own home address.

Our immediate plans are to make it even more attractive by painting the exterior, improving the landscaping, and re-designing the courtyard.

We also plan to visit with each of you to check your apartment for any necessary maintenance work -- especially plumbing or electrical. This work will also be scheduled soon after May 1st -- with priority to problems of the most urgency.

We purchase and maintain our buildings on a pride of ownership basis. We appreciate our tenants and respect your rights to live in a clean well-kept building. We will do everything within reason so that you too may take pride in your home.

All checks for rent in advance due on or after May 1st should be made payable to

JOSEPH SCHWARTZ

The manager is authorized to collect rents as heretofore.

We are happy to have you as tenants and we hope to continue a pleasant relationship for years to come.

Thank you for your consideration and cooperation during the renovating period.

Sincerely,

J Schwartz

Chapter XI

PRESENT TENANTS

or

presents for tenants

You are now the proud owner of an apartment house. You are in business just as though you had a furniture or appliance store. You must look upon tenants as customers. You must also appreciate that when the building is fully rented you do not have to open your store for business—you can remain closed. You have no advertising expense, no clerks, no solicitation, no business expense. However, when a vacancy does occur you must open your shop—hire clerks, advertise and solicit. Therefore, you have an incentive to keep your customers happy.

Why operate your business so that you keep losing customers, only to have to go to the expense of looking for a customer replacement. If you have 12 apartments, you need only 12 tenants. If you operate your building slovenly and treat your tenants poorly, causing three vacancies during the year, you are forced to look for three new tenants—but your total still remains 12, not 15. What have you accomplished? You are going backwards; and many owners are doing just that and do not realize it. They and their managers ignore the cost of constant tenant turnover and instead point with pride that they have secured new tenants quite promptly and, I might add, quite often. Therefore, the first, second, third, and only rule is select *good stable tenants.*

Hold on to your present customers, keep them happy even though you might have to redecorate a present tenant's apartment. Wow, I said it. I said a terrible thing; something that apartment house owners don't even dare think of—redecorate a present tenant's apartment. No apartment house owner ever hesitates decorating a vacant apartment to attract a new tenant. This irritates the five-year tenant, who has not had his apartment painted since the day he moved in. You should offer to redecorate the apartment of every two-or-more-year tenant that you wish to maintain. If you do, he will remain a tenant for another two or three years. I have offered to repaint a number of occupied tenant's apartments, but a year or more passes before they request it because they do not want to go through the disturbance of moving furniture and having painters under foot. However, knowing that I have offered to redecorate, they are no longer irritated when a vacancy is redecorated. But more important, they are not looking for another apartment as many tenants are forced to do because of the short-sighted policy of their present landlord.

The owner who has a vacancy recarpets and paints the vacant apartment, and is losing one or more months' rent between the old and the new tenant. Yet ironically he will refuse to do so for his present tenant, even though he will not lose a single days rent; and the "saved" rental income will pay for the redecorating. This is a prime example of what could be termed "owner's myopia." Don't be guilty of it.

When you find you have inherited a tenant who will not allow you to go into the apartment but will meet you at the front door to transact your business, undoubtedly that tenant is either keeping a dirty apartment that he does not want you to see, or it is damaged badly. In every instance I have found it is best for the entire building to ask that person to move. And when the person does move, I find that my fears were justified. The apartment is really in bad shape and no normal damage deposit could cover the damage repairs that we have to cope with. However, this was part of my risk and I was willing to create a vacancy in order to improve living conditions for everyone concerned. Ultimately it works to my advantage because tenants are prone to "stay put" in a well-kept apartment building where the maintainence standards are high.

When a vacancy occurs always offer your present tenants a cash amount, such as $25 or $50, if they can recommend an acceptable new tenant. (A sample letter follows which can be adapted for this purpose.) And offer the vacating tenant the return of his cleaning fee if he will cooperate and allow you to show his apartment before he moves out, if the apartment is rerented with absolutely no loss of rent. (Although all leases and agreements give the owner permission to show an apartment to a prospective tenant, unless the tenant is cooperative it is better to wait until he has moved.) Another need for a moving tenant's cooperation: It is sometimes necessary to ask the vacating tenant if he would move a few days or even a week before the end of the month, in order that the new tenant might move in on the first of the month. Your old tenant, who will be a new tenant in another building, can often get into a vacant apartment a few days before the end of the month. Any landlord will allow him that privilege and you would do the same. So offer the moving-out tenant a pro-rata rent refund if you have to. By paying the cleaning fee, and a few days, or one week pro-rata rent refund, you are giving up about 25% of the rent in order to get 100%.

Otherwise the tenant invariably moves out on the 31st of the month and you have to start painting and cleaning, which takes four or five days. The next tenant doesn't want his rent to start until the first of the following month, which means you have lost one month's rent or maybe even two.

I must repeat—for emphasis—a vacancy doesn't cost the landlord a $5, $10 or $20 bill—it costs him hundreds of dollars. This is the only business I know that takes such large losses as a matter of course, rather than change their course.

Think of this paradox: most tenants move because their apartments need repainting; the drapes are dirty and thread-bare; the shower door is cracked; the kitchen linoleum has a bare spot in front of the sink, etc. The only way to get a freshly painted, newly draped apartment is to move to another building. NOTE: this "fresh" apartment was also vacated by a tenant because it needed repainting, new drapes, etc.

"Musical chairs," but the owner is tone-deaf.

January 30, 19XX

Dear Friend:

Perhaps you have a friend who is looking for an apartment.

We have a vacancy at 120 Main Street -- a 2 bedroom upper which rents for $230 per month (no pets -- one child considered).

Naturally we would favor tenants who are known favorably to preferred occupants such as yourself.

If a tenant is secured through your recommendation, I will be pleased to present you with a $25 gift certificate.

The apartment is in process of being made ready but can be seen now.

Be sure to give me or the Manager your friend's name *before* he looks at the apartment -- in order that you might be credited as the sponsor.

Thank you.

Sincerely,

Joseph Schwartz

Chapter XII

VACANCY SIGNS

or

stopping traffic

It is standard practice to place a sign outside of the building to attract attention to your vacancy, and this brings me to the subject of signs and the stupidity that surrounds this subject.

Why should you have a sign saying *apartment* for rent? Anyone can see it is an apartment building. And yet I have seen many buildings with permanent signs stating "Apartment for Rent, 1, 2, and 3 bedrooms." Then it says, "Carpets, Drapes, Built-Ins, Air, Pool," etc. Most people looking for apartments are cruising about in autos, especially in most areas like California. A motorist cannot read all of this comprehensive sign. If you have a vacancy just say, "2 Bedroom, 2 Bath, Unfurnished." That is all that is necessary.

This can be in large letters so people can read it as they pass by in their car. Incidentally, a colorful pennant or two stuck in the lawn is also very helpful. If the apartment can be shown, always put up a sign saying *OPEN*. It will bring many a looker who had previously stopped at buildings with "vacancy" signs but there was no manager or the apartment was occupied and could not be shown. Signs with the one word *OPEN* are the most effective of all.

All signs should be professionally painted. No amateurish home-made signs. And if the building is filled up, why have any sign at all. I am thoroughly against the practice of displaying permanent (never-take-down) signs describing the entire building and then having that small sign on it saying "SORRY—NO VACANCY." Either say "Happy—No Vacancy," or better yet, say nothing.

The best looking building of all is the one with no signs thereon whatever, except the street number and the name of the building. Don't cheapen the appearance of your building with unnecessary signs. And when they *are* necessary, don't clutter them up with unnecessary words.

Chapter XIII

NEWSPAPER ADS

or

creating traffic

In addition to posting signs and letting your tenants know that you have a vacancy, you should also advertise in your local paper. If there is a neighborhood throw-away, it is far more effective than any other paper because it is localized. And when you advertise, be sure to spend the money for an extra few words, such as, describing *the size of the building.* For example, your ad should read "2 bedroom, 2 bath in an *8 unit* custom-built building." The "8 unit" will draw more attention than the fact that you have a 2 bedroom, because many people wish to move from their 30 or 40 unit apartment building to a smaller building. They wish to get away from the cold, impersonal, hotel-type building to the small, warm, neighborly type. Many of our new tenants tell us that the size of our building in the newspaper was what caused them to come to see—and not incidentally, over 50% of our new tenants are directly attributable to newspaper ads.

Obviously, I do not use newspaper ads often, but when I do, my ad is almost invariably the only one in the entire classified section that spells out the size of the building. Check your paper and see if you can find any "6 units, 8 units, or 12 units" mentioned. As soon as this book is distributed, the newspapers will get increased revenue but it will cost the advertiser less because he will rent his apartment sooner.

In the ad, always give the address of the building. Do not just advertise a phone number. Many prospective tenants wish to check the exterior and locality of the building, just as I suggested you do when you go looking to purchase a building. They also like to get addresses and cruise about to decide whether or not they wish to go to the bother of looking at the interior of the building. So it is your job to keep the exterior looking attractive enough so they will wish to see the interior.

Inquiries by phone are always from the best prospective tenants. They will ask about pets, children, size of bedrooms, dining area, etc. If they follow up with a visit, you have an excellent chance to make a sale. So don't ignore the phone calls—they are serious—and foot-weary.

Chapter XIV

APPLICATION TO RENT

or

who gets the keys?

Prospective tenants should all be required to complete a comprehensive "Application to Rent" form. This application should preferably be a form that is supplied by the Apartment House Association so that people will realize it is a standard form in general use, and not one you alone require. A typical form is reproduced on the following page by special permission of the Apartment Owners Association of San Fernando Valley.

APPLICATION TO RENT

Name _____ Age _____ Social Security or Employment No. _____ Drivers License No. _____

Name _____ Age _____ Social Security or Employment No. _____ Drivers License No. _____

PROPOSED OCCUPANTS	RELATIONSHIP	AGE	OCCUPATION

Will you have any pets? _____ If so, describe _____

Why are you vacating your present place of residence? _____

Give the following information as to your last three places of residence:

Address	Rent Paid	Name of Owner or Manager	Phone	From - to Date
present				
last previous				

Current Salary Range $ _____ Monthly $ _____ or Annual $ _____

	Present Occupation	Prior Occupation	Spouse's Occupation
Occupation			
Employer			
Business Address			
Business Phone			
Position held			
Name & Title of Superior			
How long?			

Do you maintain a Bank Account? _____ Commercial or Savings? _____ Account No. _____

Name of Bank	Branch	Address

Financial Obligations:

Payments to:	Address	Amount
Payments to:	Address	Amount
Payments to:	Address	Amount

Personal Reference	Address	Phone	Length of Acq'ce	Occupation

Nearest Relative	Address	Phone	City	Relationship

Automobile - Make _____ Model _____ Year _____ License Number _____

Applicant represents that statements above made are true and correct and hereby authorizes verification of references and agrees to furnish additional credit references on request.

The undersigned makes application to rent housing accommodations designated as:

Apt. No. _____ Located at _____

The rental for which is $ _____ per _____ and upon approval of this application agrees to sign rent or lease agreement in the form hereto attached.

Dated: _____ ,19 ___

_____ Applicant

Time: _____

_____ Applicant

I have instructed my managers not to accept any deposits at the time the Application to Rent is completed. My reasoning is that we avoid the problem of returning the deposit to an unacceptable tenant—our turn-down can be handled entirely by phone. If the tenant is acceptable, I feel that he will be around to give us a deposit after our acceptance. Otherwise, if he has changed his mind while waiting for our credit check, then he wasn't 100% sold in the first place. It is interesting that obviously undesirable tenants will sometimes insist on our taking such a deposit. If we must, then we use an "Advance Deposit Receipt" (pages 72-73).

Every Application to Rent is submitted to the Apartment House Association for a credit check. This is not fool-proof for it cannot be a guarantee of a good tenant, but it can prevent you from getting involved with guaranteed bad tenants. The cost is negligible compared to the benefits, and I apply for credit checks even on what appears to be obviously bad or obviously good applicants, for I have been wrong on occasion.

In addition, I have many times checked their former addresses to see the type of building or neighborhood they lived in, and in some cases I have interviewed the former managers.

No matter how well-groomed or how soft-spoken the prospective tenant might be, if he balks at the completion of the application, that person usually turns out to be an undesirable tenant. Most often the person who will not give checking account or charge card information is a bad credit risk. My experience has been that no one who has checked out well has ever made any objection whatever to the application form. Actually they seem to appreciate that we are selective. However, completion of the application without objection is not always dependable, because many an application that I thought acceptable proved, upon investigation, to be a "no! no!" And in every instance that he said "Don't phone me, I'll call you," he has never called us and he was always unacceptable. Surprisingly, whenever I have notified a prospective tenant that we are not approving his application, I have never had any repercussions because of our disapproval.

Save all of your Applications to Rent, and the credit reports also. Especially save all turn-downs; you may need them some day to prove that this is a regular requirement of yours.

Although you may have been very selective, your new tenant may prove to be an alcoholic, a swinger, a wife beater. As soon as you know it, kick him out. It won't get any better, so take your beating now. It will avoid upsetting other tenants and they will respect you for it. I recall one building where the first one of our many vacancies was rented to tenants that were objectionable within 48 hours. The tenant's friends came visiting at all hours of the night and were noisy and offensive. It was not the tenants, but their friends, yet I promptly notified the tenants to move. I offered to return all of their deposits and the pro-rata rent so they moved within six days. The effect on the other tenants was most beneficial. Here was a new owner taking over a building with vacancies, and yet he did not hesitate to create another vacancy. The faster you act, the better.

Remember that you still (as of the date of this printing) have the right to reject an applicant because he has pets, children, a 10 ton truck, a souped-up motorcycle, etc. Even those rights may be taken away—and when they go, I think I will go, too.

ADVANCE DEPOSIT RECEIPT

Subject to approval by the undersigned Landlord, or agent, of the Applicant and his submitted Application to Rent Apt. No. ...., located at ....
.... in the city of ....
and subject further to the stated premises being vacated by the present occupants, the sum of $........... is accepted to secure their rental for occupancy by .... adults and .... children, as listed below:

....

The agreed beginning date of rental will be ....
at the rate of $........... a month, payable in advance on the .... day of each month. The applicant also acknowledges that Landlord will require a Security Deposit of $........... and an earned non-refundable Cleaning Fee of $..........., making a total amount due before occupancy of $.............

In the event of approval of Applicant by Landlord and vacation of premises by present occupants, the amount of this deposit shall apply to the first month's rent. However, if Applicant does not return on or before ....(a.m./p.m.) on the date of .... to claim the accommodations in question by paying the balance of $........... due under this agreement, and completing all other forms or agreements, as itemized ...., this deposit shall be retained by the Landlord as liquidated damages, and Applicant waives all right to occupancy, giving his permission for the Landlord to immediately rent the premises to another party without notice of such rental.

If the Application to Rent is not approved by the Landlord or if the premises in question cannot be offered to the Applicant for his occupancy on the specified date, then Applicant agrees to accept the return of the stated sum of deposit in full and complete satisfaction of any claim he may have because of the said deposit or by reason of any completed rental, lease, or other agreements.

....
Applicant

....
Date

....
Applicant

....
Landlord

Form No. 101 - Apt. Own. Assn. - S.F.V.

Chapter XV

LEASES OR AGREEMENTS

or

sign on "what" bottom line

The common meaning of the word "lease" in the apartment business is "an agreement for a year or more—with first and last month's rent paid in advance." So when a prospective tenant sees a sign saying "Apartment for Lease," he is expected to know that the landlord is looking for a long term tenant—at least one year. There is usually no cleaning fee or damage deposit required.

The word "rent" is usually used to indicate a month-to-month tenancy with both parties free to terminate the tenancy with one month's notice. In this case, the last month's rent in advance is rarely asked for, but there almost always are cleaning fees and damage (or security) deposits.

I do not use leases because a tenant can always walk away from his lease whereas the owner cannot. I am not an attorney and I am not saying this in a legal sense. I am an owner and I am saying this in a practical sense. And when the tenant breaks his lease, he always uses up his last month's rent, so I have nothing to offset against any damage to the apartment.

I use a month-to-month agreement in every instance. In fact, I have never used a lease. With a month-to-month agreement for a $200 monthly rental I can ask for and receive a $50 cleaning fee and a $100 damage (or security) deposit. Incidentally, I have only had two tenants move out where I kept the damage deposits (in my 12-year landlord experience), and in both instances the deposits did not cover the damage incurred. If I had a copy of this book before those tenants moved in, they would never have moved in.

The deposits are justified because if the tenant discovers he does not enjoy living in my building he can move out at the end of the second month. He can get his $100 damage deposit provided there is no damage and he can even get his $50 cleaning fee if he will clean the apartment, the windows, the bathrooms, the rugs, and leave it spotlessly clean as he found it. In most instances they prefer to ignore the cleaning fee. If they have lived here only a few months (as in the case of an unexpected transfer of employment), they are embarrassed by their short stay even though they might leave the premises in an immaculate condition; and if they have lived here three or four years, they won't clean the apartment for a return of only $50. Nor can I get it done for $50 either.

The owners who require two or three year leases usually sell the long term commitment by giving the 13th or 25th month rent-free. The month-to-month tenant doesn't expect any rent concessions. He is easier to sell on a short term commitment and he pays his full rent for the same two or three year period.

So let us compare the two agreements as follows:

	LEASE	MONTH-TO-MONTH AGREEMENT
Quality of tenant	Same	Same
Down payment on $200 Rental	$400	$350
Obligation of Landlord	1 (or 2) years	30 days
Obligation of Tenant	*30 days	30 days
$ Recovery by Landlord	Nothing	$50 to $150

Will Rogers once said, "I never met a man that I did not like." I say, "I never saw a month-to-month agreement that I liked—entirely."

So I made up my own form by borrowing, stealing, copying, editing, and adding—had it set in type and printed. After much time, expense, and experience using my "perfect" form, I found a much better one (Form 107) printed by the Apartment Service Co. With their permission I am reproducing the form.

---

*NOTE: If you are using leases—although tenant has signed a one, two, or three year lease, he might *at any time* stop paying rent and tell you that he is using up his last month's advance—and you will do nothing to enforce the lease, I'll betcha!

APARTMENT RENTAL AGREEMENT

(Month to Month Tenancy — Furnished or Unfurnished)

THIS RENTAL AGREEMENT shall evidence the terms under which the parties whose signatures appear below and are identified as Landlord and Tenant, respectively, do hereby agree on the part of Landlord to rent to Tenant, and on the part of Tenant to rent from Landlord, the premises herein described under the following terms and conditions:

1. PREMISES: Apartment No. _____, located at _____

in the City of _____ and State of _____

Assigned Parking Area No. _____ Assigned Storage Area No. _____

2. TERM AND RENTAL: The term of this rental agreement shall commence at 12:01 A.M. on the _____ day of

_____, 19____, and shall be for a tenancy from month-to-month at a rental of _____

_____ dollars ($ _____) per month payable in advance on or before the _____

day of each month at the office or apartment of the manager or owner of the building.

3. OTHER CHARGES: Landlord acknowledges receipt of the following agreed amounts: Cleaning Charge $ _____,
Key Deposit $ _____, Security Deposit $ _____. The key deposit and security deposit are to be returned to
Tenant at the termination of this agreement upon redelivery of all keys and premises to Landlord, less any damages to
the premises, fixtures or furnishings and any other amount due under this agreement. The cleaning charge is a one-time
charge to compensate Landlord for the cost of preparing the apartment for rental and as consideration for entering into
this agreement. It is not refundable at any time. Tenant is to pay when due any utility or other charge accruing in connection with the use of the premises except for the following, which are to be paid by Landlord: _____

_____ A late fee of $ _____ shall be added to any payment of rent not made
before three days after the due date or for which a deficient check shall have been given.

4. OCCUPANTS: Regular occupants of the premises shall be restricted to those parties who have signed this agreement and the following named individuals: _____
The stay of any other person shall not exceed one week without authorization of Landlord or his agent. Tenant shall
pay additional rent for the period of stay of any unauthorized occupant at a rate of $ _____ per month and
acceptance of such payment by Landlord shall not waive any requirement of this agreement.

5. CONDITION OF PREMISES: By executing this agreement, Tenant acknowledges that he has received the premises
and such appliances, furniture, furnishings or other contents as may be provided therewith, including but not restricted
to those items listed on the inventory herein and finds them to be in good and clean condition and repair except as may be
indicated elsewhere in this agreement. Tenant agrees to take good care of the premises and its contents, to commit no
waste on or about the premises, and at the termination of this agreement to return the premises and its contents clean and
free from trash and in the same condition as when received except for such ordinary wear and tear as reasonable and careful
use would have caused.

6. USE OF PREMISES: a. *Noise* — All activities of Tenant or those of his guests or occupants are to be conducted in a quiet, dignified manner so as not to annoy or disturb other tenants or create a nuisance in any way. b. *Unlawful Activities* — Tenant agrees not to use the premises for any commercial enterprise or for any purpose which is unlawful, against city ordinances, or which would injure the reputation of the building or its occupants in any way. c. *Animals* — No animal, bird or pet of any kind may be kept on or about the premises without the written permission of Landlord or his agent. d. *Alterations* — No change of locks, installation of aerials, lighting fixtures or other equipment, use of nails, screws or fastening devices on walls, ceiling or woodwork, or alteration or redecoration of the premises is to be made without prior written authorization of Landlord or his agent. e. *Cleaning and Refuse* — Tenant shall keep the premises, and its equipment and contents in a reasonably clean and neat condition at all times. All refuse and garbage shall be deposited by Tenant in the proper receptacles as provided and Tenant shall cooperate in keeping the refuse area neat. Tenant shall be responsible for disposing of articles of such size or nature as are not acceptable by the rubbish hauler for the building. f. *Mechanical Equipment* — Automobiles, motorcycles or other mechanical equipment may be parked only in such space as may be assigned to Tenant and are not to be washed or disassembled on or near the general premises. g. *Exterior Display* — No signs, laundry or articles of any kind are to be hung or displayed by Tenant on the exterior of the premises except for laundry in an authorized laundry drying area. h. *Loitering* — Lounging or unnecessary loitering in the halls or on the front steps or public balconies in such a way as to interfere with the convenience of other tenants is prohibited. i. *House, Pool and Laundry Rules* — Tenant shall comply with such house, pool or laundry rules as may be posted from time to time on the general premises. Rights of usage to the pool area or laundry room are conditioned upon reasonable and careful use and are gratuitous subject to revocation by Landlord at any time for any reason.

7. DAMAGES: Tenant shall promptly pay for any damage to the premises, general premises, contents, furnishings and equipment thereof which may be caused by Tenant, his guests or occupants. Drains and waste pipes are acknowledged to have been clear at commencement of this agreement unless reported otherwise to Landlord within one week therefrom and the cost of clearing any partial or complete stoppage occurring during the term of this agreement shall be paid by Tenant.

8. ABANDONMENT OR ASSIGNMENT: Tenant covenants that he will occupy the premises continuously except for normal vacation periods and agrees that any absence therefrom for more than one week, during any part of which time rental is delinquent or during which time the tenant shall have removed the major part of his belongings, shall be conclusively presumed to be an abandonment of the premises at the option of the Landlord and shall entitle the Landlord to take possession and re-rent the premises. Tenant agrees not to transfer, assign or sublet the premises or any part thereof and hereby authorizes Landlord as his agent to evict any other person claiming possession by way of assignment or subletting under his authority or this agreement.

9. RESPONSIBILITY OF OWNER: a. *Right of Entry* — Landlord or his agent, by himself or with others, shall have the right to enter the premises at any time for the purpose of examining or repairing the same, showing the premises to prospective tenants or purchasers, or enforcing any lien provided for under any State or Federal law or this agreement. b. *Loss or Theft* — Landlord shall not be responsible for loss, injury or damage to the personal property or person of Tenant, his guests or occupants, caused directly or indirectly by acts of God, fire, theft, burglary, malicious acts, riot, insurrection, civil commotion, the elements, defects in the building, furnishings, equipment, outside stairways, walks or landscaping, or by the neglect of other tenants or owners of contiguous property. c. *Defects and Repairs* — Sections 1941 and 1942 of the California Civil Code are waived. No defect in the premises, furnishings or equipment shall constitute grounds for offset, abatement or reduction of rent or entitle Tenant to terminate this agreement. d. *Possession* — In the event Landlord is unable to deliver possession of the premises on the commencement date of this agreement or as agreed, because of the loss or destruction of the premises or because of the failure of the prior tenant to vacate or for any other reason, the

agreed rental shall abate until the actual date of possession or the Landlord may return all prior payments to Tenant and cancel this agreement without further obligation to Tenant in any way.

10. DEFAULT: If any default in the payment of rent or in any other term of this agreement is not cured within 3 days after notice of such default is given Tenant, or if Tenant shall breach this agreement, commit a nuisance or abandon the premises, Landlord may repossess the premises and forthwith terminate this agreement without further notice and Tenant shall promptly surrender the premises and pay to Landlord all sums to which he may be entitled, including damages, reasonable attorney's fees and any other expense caused by such default or in regaining possession of the premises. Acceptance of rent by Landlord after any default shall not be construed to waive any right of Landlord or affect any notice or legal action theretofore given or commenced.

In addition to any other rights or remedies to which he may be entitled, Landlord shall have a lien upon any property of Tenant located on the premises or in the possession of Landlord to secure the payment of any sums which may be due under this agreement, which lien may be enforced in the same manner as that provided under Section 1861a of the California Code of Civil Procedure.

Items due under this agreement shall be immediately payable and if not paid within five days from due date Landlord may add the amount as rental to be paid on the next rental payment date.

11. RENEWAL OR TERMINATION: a. *Automatic Renewal* — This agreement is automatically renewed from month to month but may be terminated at any time by either party giving to the other in writing 30 days prior notice of intention to terminate. No oral notice or notice given by Tenant under which the termination date is not definite or Tenant does not completely vacate the premises including all storage areas within the said 30 days shall be effective. b. *Holding Over* — It is understood that fulfillment of the requirements of such notice of termination on or before the termination date is essential to permit Landlord to re-rent the premises or prepare for re-rental on a definite date and it is therefore agreed between the parties that should Tenant hold over the premises beyond the termination date or fail to vacate on or before the termination date, the rental for such period shall be twice the normal amount and Lessee shall be liable for such other damages through loss of prospective tenant or otherwise as Landlord may suffer due to such holding over. c. *Termination Procedure* — Upon termination — (1) Tenant shall completely vacate the premises, including any storage or other areas of the general premises which he may be occupying or have goods stored therein. (2) Tenant shall also deliver all keys, personal property listed on the attached inventory and all personal property furnished for Tenant's use during the term of this agreement, whether or not listed on the inventory, to Landlord in good, clean and sanitary condition, reasonable wear and tear excepted. (3) Before departure, Tenant shall leave his forwarding address and shall allow Landlord or his agent to inspect the premises in Tenant's presence to verify the final condition of the premises and its contents.

12. PERIOD OF RENTAL: Tenant represents that he will occupy the premises under the terms of this agreement for at least _____ months in lieu of which the Security Deposit is to be applied to the cost of re-rental and any loss due to intervening vacancy and the balance returned to Tenant.

13. OTHER COVENANT:

INVENTORY

Area	No.	Item, Description and Color	Area	No.	Item, Description and Color
Living Room			Bedroom No. 1		
			Bedroom No. 2		
			Other		
Kitchen and Dinette					

IN WITNESS WHEREOF, the parties have set their hands and seals this _____ day of _____, 19___.

LANDLORD   TENANT

By _____   By _____

                                        By _____

But even this form is not perfect for I would add (and I do, as Paragraphs 13 and 14) the following:

13. No piano, organ, or waterbed shall be moved into any apartment without permission of the owner.

14. No heavy appliances such as refrigerators shall be moved without professional movers and/or professional padded dollies so as to prevent damage to the stairs.

Chapter XVI

NEW TENANTS

or

who calls the plumber?

When a new tenant is about to move into your building, start the little extras. Make sure that every light fixture has light bulbs. Leave a bar of soap *in the original wrapper* at every water outlet. Leave toilet tissue in each bathroom *in its original wrapper*. Leave a roll of paper towels at the sink *in its original wrapper* and a few paper cups. And, if they have children, instruct the manager to call on the tenant as he is moving in to offer milk and a box of cookies for the children while they are moving. You would be surprised how many mothers forget milk and cookies for the children. Our "welcome wagon" makes quite an impression. We have had people say that they felt as though it was the Holiday Inn.

These little extras have paid off very well, and the cost is negligible.

Our month-to-month agreement clearly states that maintenance such as plugged-up plumbing is a cost of the tenant. We want no misunderstanding so we state this negative as a positive—we tell the new tenant that during the first week of tenancy, we should be advised if there are any sluggish drains or if the garbage disposal or toilets are plugged up. We tell him that we do not use his bathroom or his garbage disposal, and that a stoppage of the toilet by a child's toy or the jamming of the disposal by a teaspoon is his expense and not ours. This is important because it leaves no chance for misunderstanding. A clogged disposal or toilet is going to occur and in most instances the clogging is due to the tenant. Therefore, why not explain this fully before it happens. I find that it doesn't happen as often now that I explain this to the tenant. Apparently, they are much more careful and they are also much more apt to get the plunger and use it themselves before they call the plumber.

You may think this is "much ado about nothing." When I operated my 14 unit building as a "non-profit" tax shelter project (but it was not supposed to be non-profit), the most common, and the most urgent maintenance expense was for clogged toilets and disposals. There wasn't a single month that I missed having a plumber's bill—always the tenants fault and yet not once could I collect from the tenant. And almost always the stoppage occurs in the evenings or weekends so that the plumber charges overtime.

Now, with 28 units, I have never had to pay for a single plumber's call in the past two years. The difference is that *the owner* used to call the plumber—now it's the tenant who calls the plumber.

Buy the garbage disposal tool for freeing the jammed

disposal and also buy the faithful plunger. Tell the tenants that these tools are hanging in the laundry room and available for their use. They take care of 98% of the problems. If not, the tenant calls the plumber, who always finds a knife jammed in the disposal. The tenant pays the bill, and we hear nothing more about it. This, I maintain, is proper management. Yet in most cases this problem is ignored until it really mounts, invariably culminating in a misunderstanding between tenant and owner.

Chapter XVII

TENANT RELATIONS

or

love 'em or they leave you

A good salesman takes the time to tell his customers he remembers them—he does so regularly, inexpensively, but sincerely. For example, he sends birthday cards, and they are greatly appreciated by the customers.

So learn from the successful salesmen—send to each tenant an anniversary (of tenancy) card each year plus "MONEY." Yes, I mean MONEY. At the end of the first year send him a check for $100 (return of damage deposit). Tell him you are pleased to have him as a tenant and that you know there is no need for a damage deposit from him. If this is too drastic a step for you, at least send him $6 and tell him you are giving him 6% interest on his $100 damage deposit. Either way, you are losing nothing but are gaining much.

If the apartment is occupied by a family with children, always use the 6% interest method. I prefer to hold the damage deposit, for it is a less painful way of paying for the window that Johnny tossed the baseball through.

I do not always wait for the anniversary. A tenant asked for permission to replace the bathroom and kitchen light fixtures with flourescents. I not only gave her permission but I immediately refunded her damage deposit.

Another tenant asked for permission for additional built-in shelving in the kitchen and bathroom. The work was done by a professional cabinetmaker paid-for by the tenant and it too will remain in my building when they move. So I returned this tenant's security deposit one month after he moved in.

Get the point? If you think I returned the last two deposits because they improved my property, that's only one reason. The other and more important reason is that barring some wholly unexpected developments these tenants are probably going to stay for years and years because they put their own money into making improvements that they intend to enjoy. They could just as well have signed a five year lease.

Also, be sure to give your tenant a Christmas or Chanukah present, for he is your customer. You receive such presents from trades people because you are a good customer of theirs. Why not do the same for your customers? Spend $10 per apartment each year foolishly—and you will find it will return thousands of dollars to you plus much enjoyment.

To the owner of the building this is a business. To the tenant this is his home, a place to sleep, a place to live, a place to socialize, a place to bring up his family; this isn't just a rent receipt. Homes and families have birthdays, holidays, anniversaries. Join the family, as you wrap up a holiday gift for your tenants; and don't forget a toy for each of the children.

A letter of the type that follows can be adapted for the particular occasion.

December 1, 19XX

Dear Bill:

The payment of your December rent marks the end of your first year with us -- Happy First Anniversary. I appreciate that you and your wife have enjoyed making your home in my building and I and all the co-tenants have enjoyed having you nice folks as neighbors.

When you rented your apartment you gave me $100 as a Security Deposit for possible damage. Enclosed is a check refunding that $100 as you are the type of people that do not damage property; you improve my property by your very presence.

I hope to be privileged to have you as tenants for many more anniversaries to come.

Sincerely,

Joseph Schwartz

Chapter XVIII

THE MANAGER

or

tell him and then let him

When you take over the building tell the manager that you would like to have him remain as manager for a month until you get acquainted. Do not make any commitment until you find out whether this man is your man or not. Don't worry if he tells you that if he does not remain manager the entire building will be vacated. Many managers say that to impress the new owner but it is usually a colossal bluff. However, I do have one building where all the tenants would no doubt say the same thing because the manager is that popular. But should he be replaced, I know that most tenants will not move. Tenants will move because they do not like a manager, but most tenants will not move when the manager leaves despite their liking him.

So you are now getting acquainted, and if the manager is the type of person that you would invite to your own dinner table, fine, keep him. On the other hand, if he is not, look first at the other tenants. If you find a tenant weeding your grass or watering your lawn occasionally, tending plants out on his patio and acting as though the whole building was his own home, he has the makings of a manager.

None of my buildings requires a full-time manager. In fact, I could do without managers, as could many other owners who nevertheless employ them. There is no law requiring a manager in any of my buildings. In California, 16 units or more does require a manager. But I definitely recommend a part-time manager for all buildings from 4 units or more.

The cost for a manager is nominal. Most owners allow $5 per month per apartment for the manager's compensation. If you have an 8 unit building you allow $40 a month reduction in rent for the manager. For $40 a month the manager shows vacant apartments and collects the rents. He also does simple chores such as changing light bulbs about the grounds, and turning on the sprinklers. He does no complicated maintenance work and is not required to be on the premises 24 hours a day. You will find many of your tenants willing to accept the responsibility as manager for $35 or $40 per month. I have had absolutely no problems as far as managers are concerned. This, in my opinion, puts the lie to the experts' advice that one large building of 30 units means that you have one good manager, instead of having three part-time, poor managers in three small buildings. I tell you that my managers are good. They are good tenants which qualifies them as excellent managers. And my managers are good because they manage the tenants as neighbors, so that the buildings do not require management. In contrast, the 30 or 40 unit building requires constant building management, because of the continual tenant turnover caused by poor management of tenants and by inept, disinterested ownership.

Any work that my managers perform beyond the minor chores calls for extra compensation. If they wish to clean an apartment, they get paid for it. However, a professional cleaner usually does a better job than the amateur, and I prefer that my managers do not clean apartments. If the manager wishes to paint an apartment, and he is not employed elsewhere, I might allow him to do so. However, I might lose a month's rent if he takes too long, so here too I would rather use a professional. To sum up: Never get yourself committed to allow the manager to do all the maintenance work and never lose sight of the fact that you are the owner and therefore the one to tell the manager what he can or cannot do. Never pay a manager more than what you would have to pay a professional. In fact, you should pay less. You will often find that the manager has a wrong impression of the cost for painting, cleaning and shampooing. When he finds out what the professional charges, the manager will no longer be as anxious to do the work.

Compare this to a 14 unit building owned by a Group II syndicate where the manager gets a 2 bedroom apartment (worth $175) plus $250 monthly salary. He is supposed to do all the maintenance, including gardening, painting and cleaning apartments, rug shampooing, etc. In one such case, I heard that the manager quit because he still felt the landlord expected too much work for too little money. I would have allowed the manager $70 a month towards his rent, hired a gardener, hired a professional painter, cleaner, shampooer, and the work would have been much better for much less expense.

The personality of the building is going to reflect your own personality. You are going to have an immediate effect on that building's tenancy personality—for better or for worse. The first step is to select the right manager; the same type of person that you want as a tenant. If the building is "Adults Only," your managers should be adults with no children. If the building is to be a family building with children, you should have a manager with children. He will not only appreciate that children have to make some noise, but he will be *tolerant and understanding*. A couple would not, and they would be forever in the tenant's hair complaining about the children.

The manager is your agent. Give him your picture of a desirable tenant. Tell him that he is to try to secure only the type of tenant that he would not mind having at his own dinner table. Give him the responsibility and place in him your complete confidence. Explain to him that he cannot reject any person who wishes to make an application, because under present anti-discriminatory laws every refusal is suspect. And make certain that he understands the equal housing provision guaranteed under the Civil Rights Act of 1968. Otherwise you are going to be in trouble. Don't hire a bigot. Impress upon the manager that his job is not to rent every apartment immediately, but to rent them to people who might be permanent tenants. You do not want apartment hoppers. Let him know that you would rather keep an apartment vacant for a month than to allow a possible problem tenant to move in.

Chapter XIX

MAINTENANCE

or

m-a-i-n-t-e-n-a-n-t-s

Maintenance of an apartment building can be greatly simplified. Immediately after purchasing the building, take note of all of the appliances, such as built-in ovens, ranges, air conditioners, even the plumbing fixtures, toilets and sinks. Write down the manufacturer's name and model number for each item; and not just the large appliances. It is just as important to know that it is a Sterling faucet or an Olson, Standard, or Western toilet bowl. Then you, the owner, must locate the suppliers of parts for each appliance. The easiest way is to go through the classified yellow pages of the telephone book and find the factory branch. Phone and ask who in your area has the parts for each of these appliances. This will take a great deal of time, but it will pay off.

When you take over a five or ten year old building, you will discover that an oven handle is missing, an air conditioner knob is gone, the oven calibrated dial (showing oven temperature of 100, 200 or 300 degrees) is missing, the bathroom ventilating fan motor is burnt out, the grill on one of the air conditioners is badly damaged, and so on. These minor items can be a major problem for you and a constant irritation to the tenant until you know where to get these parts. In most instances you will be told, as I was, that you cannot get them. The hardware store doesn't carry them and the "authorized" distributor is quick to tell you that you must replace the entire unit. Even for appliances which are only five to ten years old you will often find, as I did, that you have to go all the way to the factory to get a simple knob—in my case, that meant all the way to Tennessee. Otherwise, you are faced with the utterly ridiculous alternative (as I was) of purchasing a new oven for $200 because of a missing temperature calibrated knob which is worth $1.50. (Ridiculous, you think, but the oven cannot operate correctly without that knob.) The local distributors just do not carry all the parts. You will be frustrated when they tell you that the model number is no longer being manufactured; every model over ten years of age is obsolete. This is not so, if you will contact the factory.

I've had a number of interesting experiences, such as writing to the factory of Minneapolis Honeywell in order to find a plastic cover for one of their thermostats. I was told locally by their own factory distributors that I had to purchase the entire thermostat. I did not take that for an answer. I addressed my letter to the President of Minneapolis Honeywell. Not only did I receive two letters of apology in reply and a long distance phone call, but I also received *two* plastic covers *free of charge.* Another similar instance: It was impossible to get a motor for a bathroom ventilating fan manufactured by one of the major companies. I went to the factory authorized distributor and was told that I had to buy the complete unit for $26 for they did not sell motors separately. This was only a $26 item, but I had about twenty of these fans in the building, all of which would one day require new motors. Two of them had already burnt out, and the others would soon follow for the building was ten years old, and ten years is about the life span of a fan motor that has never been oiled or cleaned by the previous landlord who did not have the benefit of this book. I scoured the city's electric motor companies, even the rebuilt motor suppliers, but it was impossible. So I contacted the factory and immediately was handed a new motor for $5. Because I knew that I would need more in the near future, I put in a supply of one dozen such motors at the cost of approximately two complete units.

With a company as large as General Electric I have had problems in getting parts from their own company parts branch. I had to go over the branch manager's head to his superior, and in every instance I got the part that I needed.

And don't neglect the most common problem area of all, the faucets. The washers and stem valves are forever needing replacement. Know the name of the manufacturer and the model number. Put in a supply of washers, and especially the simple little O rings (which is a very thin type of a washer) which costs only pennies. This alone can solve many of your plumbing problems, and they are the most elusive rascals to find. It will take hours to line up the source of these parts, but since you are going to need them not only today but again tomorrow, you had better do your homework or you will be in trouble constantly.

Any apartment building from 6 units up should have a supply of electric light bulbs, washers, O rings, a new garbage disposal, a ventilating fan motor, etc., on hand. I know of owners who didn't have as much as a 100 watt bulb in reserve—as if they would never need a bulb replacement.

And another important tip, when you have to replace a

faucet fixture, *save the old one* since this will provide you with some replacement parts that are difficult to secure otherwise.

Encourage your tenants to ask for maintenance work as soon as it is necessary, and do the work immediately.

This is a business. Be prepared to maintain your building. If you make preparations in advance, you will not only maintain your building, but also maintain your tenants. More often than you would believe possible, a building loses good tenants because the owner is penny wise and pound foolish. For want of a washer, a tenant may be lost.

Note: In my search for buildings I have seen a few well-organized workshop areas, where the owner/operator had spare parts for many of the more common problems. He had washers, nuts, bolts, knobs, light fixtures, etc., all in bins that clearly indicated the appliances to which they were related. So be sure to inquire and you might find that much of your maintenance research has already been done.

Chapter XX

THE RENT SCHEDULE

or

who pays how much?

It is almost impossible to buy a building where the rents are standardized. One of my buildings had rentals of $130, $140, and $149 for identical apartments (even $141.50).

Study your building and set up a standard rent schedule. Although it may never at any one time be completely standardized, try to get all like apartments on a like rental basis. (Due to inflation, every time you have a vacancy you'll be off-standard and you'll have to do it all over again. But that's another story.)

There is a simple way to establish your standard. Start with the one bedroom one bath apartment. Don't worry about the rents of your nearest competitor. Your building is unique. There is no other building exactly like yours within miles. (NOTE: If yours is one of two twin buildings or one of six in a row put up by the same builder, then it shouldn't be yours, because you should never buy it unless you buy all-alike contiguous buildings.)

So establish a fair rental for the one bedroom. This will take some intelligent thinking and it is very important because your entire building will be based on this figure. Let us assume you have decided on $180 per month.

Now let us agree that an additional bedroom is worth $50, and an additional bathroom is worth $25.

Your schedule therefore is:

1 Bed	1 Bath	$180
2 Bed	1 Bath	$230
2 Bed	2 Bath	$255
3 Bed	1 Bath	$280
3 Bed	2 Bath	$305

If your base of $180 is a fair rental, the above schedule is a reasonable progression. Obviously, if there are significant differences in size or in view, in patios as compared to no patios, these will cause variances in your schedule.

I have been asked many times whether the lower is worth more than an upper in a two story structure. The higher you go in a high-rise elevator building, the more the rent, but not so in a garden-type building.

My experience is that lowers and uppers should be the same, or perhaps the upper should command a higher rent. It is true that many lookers will refuse an upper because the prospective tenant is elderly or has one or two infants. But an upper is brighter, airier, and quieter than a lower. A lower is cooler is the summer and more convenient when lugging groceries, but at night one tends to close and lock the living room windows and the bedroom windows are opened only partly so that no full-sized night prowler might get in. So there are advantages and disadvantages to both. And in case I have frightened a "lower" tenant, don't be. It's no different than a private one-story house, except it's "more better." There are far less burglaries in lower apartments than in private homes because there are neighbors in the apartment building on the other side of the common wall.

Note: I personally checked apartment rental schedules in New York and Massachusetts at the time of writing this chapter. I concluded that similar size one bedroom apartments in decent middle class locations were much higher in price—$200 to $300 in the smaller buildings; $250 to $400 in the high-rise buildings. An additional bedroom seemed to command an extra $75; and an extra bathroom at least $40. And before any Eastern landlord readers tell me that my comparative figures make them look like "bad buys," let me point out that the cost of land and the cost of construction (especially heating systems) in the East is much greater than in Southern California, so rental schedules must be affected likewise.

Below-par rentals are often a hidden plus for the new owner. In many instances (but watch out for the few exceptions) the rental income is unrealistically low because in the past many Group III sellers increased the rent only on a vacant apartment. If the seller had been a good operater (as I admit I am) he did not have many vacancies in the past few years, and his long-term tenants are always paying a lower rental (as I admit mine are). Perfect example: One building's rent schedule was $165, $175, and $185 for identical apartments. Upon study I found that tenants who had been living in the building from six to eight years were paying $165; three to five year tenants were paying $175; and one to two year tenants were paying $185. This presents an interesting problem to the new owner who purchased the building at a fair price based on the present uneven rentals. What should he do? Should he increase everyone's rent immediately to $185? Here is what I would do: Nothing—absolutely nothing. The tenants will be expecting the new owner to immediately act like one of those "damn blood-sucking landlords" and some of them will already be looking for another apartment. In the meanwhile, the owner should ignore the tenants' increases but get busy improving the property.

My philosophy is: Why upset a long-term tenant by raising his rent, thus risking creating a vacancy, losing rent for a month or two, and, when a new tenant finally is acquired, redecorating the apartment to suit him at a cost of $500 to $800. And don't forget, you bought the property at a fair price based on the present gross income.

After you own the property six months and have proven that you are spending money for maintenance and the present tenants know that you are charging more for the refurbished vacant apartments, then you are justified in asking a nominal $10 increase from the $175 tenant and a $20 increase from the $165 tenant. I agree that $185 is, in this case, the true potential rent, but by the time you get them all up to the $185 level I predict you will find it to be $200. Remember inflation? The next vacancy will go for $200 not the $185 and justifiably so. And the next—$220.

Now how do you handle rent increases? No problem at all as to vacant apartments. Always ask a higher rental than the last similar rental and you will get it easily, because the newly built apartments are constantly and currently abreast of the inflationary economy. You will always be far behind.

But how do you handle rent increases affecting your present tenants? My first rule is never raise rents more often than each year (not the first of each calendar year but after a full 12 months' tenancy). I prefer to raise rents once every two years but I cannot deny that a yearly increase is justified in these runaway inflationary times. And in my opinion, about 5% is a reasonable once-a-year increase, therefore, I operate on a 10% (approximate) increase every two years. Your tenants know that your maintenance costs are increasing, so if you continue to maintain your building properly, they will not object to these reasonable increases. If you are permitting your building to become rundown and neglecting proper maintenance—they will resent a 2% increase—and rightly so.

My second rule is never use a printed "cold" Notice Of Increase form. Every apartment association has such forms but I would only give one to a tenant that I hoped might resent it and thus move out of my building.

I recommend a personal letter from you to the tenant. Let him know you are sorry to have to raise his rent. He is a customer, he pays you a lot of money and you want to keep him as a customer, so tell him so.

Following is a copy of a suggested letter. And it is even better if written in longhand rather than typewritten.

November 26, 19XX

Dear Mr. Jones:

I have tried to maintain the present rent schedule in the face of increasing costs. I appreciate that your costs have also increased. Your rent has remained at the same level for the past two years and I hope you will agree that a $20 increase is fair under the present circumstances.

Now I am sorry but I must go to more formal legal language to comply with the Rental Agreement and the 30 day written notice requirement. (By the way, I am giving you *60* days notice.)

This is to advise you that the Rental Agreement under which you hold possession of the premises known as Apartment 9 is changed effective February 1, 19XX as follows: On and after said date the rent for said apartment will be one-hundred ninety ($190) per month payable in advance.

All other terms of the Rental Agreement remain in effect as heretofore.

Sincerely,

Joseph Schwartz

Chapter XXI

ACTUAL CASH FLOW

or

in pocket, that is

Obviously, the first thing you must do is to open up a new checking account exclusively for each building. You must deposit an initial fund to operate the building. This fund must cover all the one-time capital improvements such as roof repair, painting the exterior, landscaping, cementing the patio, gutters, fences, screens, replacement of broken windows, etc. All of this should be considered as part of, and added to, the price you paid for the building. Do not consider these items to be charged against the current operations for they will completely distort your projection of the true cash flow possibilities of the building.

Deposit into that checkbook all rental income. Never co-mingle this with your personal account. Use only this checkbook to pay out all of the expenses for that building. This becomes your complete, perfect bookkeeping system. My checkbooks are all I need for income tax purposes. I have been checked by IRS a number of times and in every instance my checkbooks have been accepted as proof.

At the end of the first year (12 months after taking over) go through your checkbook. Deduct all of the monies that you have deposited other than rental income, and then see whether or not the balance has increased. In other words, let us assume that you started out with $5,000—you estimated $1,000 for an advance for current operational expenses and $4,000 for painting the exterior and other major improvements, so the total of your own money in that checkbook for the first year was $5,000. Let us also assume that you spent exactly $4,000 for the one-time capital improvements. At the end of your first 12 months if your checkbook has more than your working fund of $1,000, the excess is *cash flow*. If this figure is $1,800, you have cash flow of $800—*plus* the payments on your mortgage principal, your tax credits due to depreciation, and interest payments.

You purchased the building with the expectation of a 10% return on the money you have actually invested in that building (10% cash flow return). You will rarely achieve 10% the first year because of the vacancies that you had to absorb, but do not worry. But you better get it the second year, or you haven't managed the building very well and you should begin to worry. Again: cash flow of money invested means that if you paid $25,000 down payment and deposited and spent $4,000 for capital improvements, you have invested a total of $29,000. A 10% cash flow return is obviously $2,900. Therefore, in this case, at least after 24 months your checking account should be increased by $2,900. If you have accomplished this, then you are successful. You may now withdraw the $1,000 that you had advanced, as the building will carry itself from now on.

Most "experts" will tell you that it is impossible to expect a 10% cash flow return. Yes, this is impossible if you have a large building with perpetual vacancies, if you are a disinterested absentee owner, if you have an impersonal manager, if you are operating the building merely for tax shelter.

It is also impossible even in a smaller building with proper management, if you buy the building with only 10% down and are paying on a second and/or third mortgage. This you can do if you are a young person and have plenty of time to operate a building and do not need any cash flow. But if you are retired or are about to retire, you should not purchase any building unless you pay at least 25% of the purchase price as the down payment so that you may expect some cash flow to add to your retirement income.

The smaller buildings of 8, 10, or 12 units have another plus which helps the cash flow situation tremendously. Instead of the 10% vacancy factor, these buildings can often go through an entire year with no vacancies, and practically no maintenance. Therefore, it is possible to get the 10% cash flow easier on these buildings than on the larger ones.

Compare this with the professional investment groups who emphasize tax shelter and depreciation—not cash flow. For example, following is a formula given to me by a professional who makes up syndicates of individuals to purchase large apartment buildings:

Formula as to % of Gross Rental Income

For debt payments (mortgages including principal)	not more than	45%
For maintenance & rehabilitation each year		10%
Vacancy		10%
Resident manager		5%
Utilities		4%
Taxes		18%
Services, such as gardener, pool, rubbish, etc.		2%
Insurance		1%
Outside manager		5%
	TOTAL	**100%**

Any building that checks out within this formula is considered acceptable to this firm (who, incidentally, are to be the "outside managers"). Notice: no profit, no cash flow. Actually there is some profit even in this horrible formula for the principal payments each year do increase the equity. But where is the return on the initial investment? Now check my small building against that formula. Delete 5% for the outside manager; reduce the maintenance by 5%; reduce the vacancy by 5%; reduce resident manager to 3%. The total savings is 17% of gross rental income. This is your cash flow and, when compared to your total investment, it should be close to 10%.

And the smaller well-operated buildings will have no vacancies whatever two out of every three years. Result: the 5% vacancy factor is 0 and when 5% of rental income is added to your cash flow it should be well over 10%.

Badly operated small or large buildings can have as much as 100% turnover in one year.

Chapter XXII

LAUNDRY ROOM

or

it all comes out in the wash

Laundry services must be provided for every building, regardless of its size. An adult building of 4, 6 or 8 units will not generate enough revenue to pay for the maintenance of the equipment and the gas, electricity and water expenses. Therefore, the laundry room is a loss item in many of the small buildings. However, the cost for the gas, electric and water has already been allowed for in your estimate of utility expenses and it is minor compared to the necessity of providing this convenience.

Many owners own their laundry equipment and delude themselves in thinking that the privilege of opening the coin boxes and counting the quarters and dimes is a profitable operation. For the few owners who are mechanically inclined and who can service the machines themselves, this might be acceptable. But for the majority, the leasing of the equipment with no or very little participation in the coin receipts is by far the better course to follow.

Laundry leasing companies usually give the apartment building owner from 25% to 40% of the receipts, but they must generate at least $10 gross income each month for each piece of equipment. The minimum equipment is one washer and one dryer, therefore, the minimum gross income is $20 per month. Many small buildings do not come up to the minimum. Therefore, you should be pleased if you can arrange to lease equipment even with no participation in the receipts.

One of the buildings I purchased had a washer and dryer which was owned by the seller so I inherited the equipment. For six months I was emptying the coin boxes and I was swamped with from $14 to $20 in coins each month. I had also inherited a full service maintenance agreement with the manufacturer which cost $8.75 per month. But I was enjoying the laundry business as I hoarded the coins from my very own slot machines. One day the washer broke down, but this did not faze me a bit. I phoned the service department and was told it would be repaired on Tuesday; but this was Thursday. So Thursday, Friday, Saturday, Sunday, Monday—no laundry service. Try to explain the delay to the tenants. Finally, Tuesday arrived and I was back in business. That month my slots only paid off $6; the next month $8. And then an increase in my service agreement to $12 a month. I then realized you can't beat the slots. I phoned the St. Vincent de Paul Society and donated a washer and dryer. The leasing company did me a favor by putting in their equipment and I get no percentage whatever. It has been three years. Whenever there is a breakdown the leasing company is on the spot within an hour. The revenue is up to $20 to $25 a month, but they are entitled to it all. My tenants are happy, and I am happy to be out of the laundry business.

When I purchased an 8 unit, adult building, I did not wait to count the coins. I offered the leasing company the same deal providing they installed new equipment and providing they painted the laundry room a sparkling white.

I have since realized that the first change that a new owner can effect is to rehabilitate the laundry room, and it is the most effective way to announce that new ownership means improvement. Therefore, when I purchased my 13 unit building which had leased equipment in a dirty, dingy laundry room, I had new leased equipment installed and the laundry room repainted within 48 hours of my taking over. Incidentally, the first month's gross income from this building's laundry equipment was $14; the second was $29; the third month $43; and from then on well over the $10 minimum per piece of equipment. On this building, I am receiving 35% of the monthly receipts which probably just about covers my gas, electric and water expenses.

Chapter XXIII

POOL

or

too hot or too cold

A pool is like a convertible auto: you've got to have one once—and once is enough.

I am not prejudiced, I just don't like pools.

If your building has a pool, don't knock it—and don't fill it up and convert it to a rose garden as you will often be tempted to do.

A pool will often give you more problems than all the other building problems combined. For example, you have an adult building but adults have grandchildren who come to visit. On a beastly hot day, grandma invites the kids to swim. What do you do? Nothing—for grandma is a delightful tenant. The following week the same thing happens only this time another tenant complains. Now, what do you do?

Another example, the pool is too warm for one tenant—and too cold for another.

Another and quite serious problem. One tenant is a "polar bear"—a swimming fanatic who likes to swim no matter what the weather might be. I kept my pool heated all year long for three years because of one such tenant. Now, after a replacement of one pool heater and *one tenant*, I shut the heat off in October until June each year and save from $60 to $80 per month. This is the only problem that I can offer to solve for you. Write in the lease "Pool is heated from June 15th to October 10th." I have a friend who lives in a 30 unit building. The building was taken over by a syndicate and managed by a super-dooper professional management company. They shut off the pool heater in October. My friend (a polar bear) protested and pointed to his three year lease which referred to the pool. The management company brushed this off by stating that it did not say "heated pool." My friend produced a polaroid photo of the permanent sign affixed to the building which listed all the features of the building, including in large print "HEATED POOL." Result—the pool is heated all year long.

Although I prefer buildings without pools, I realize that a pool is attractive to many tenants. I will not reject a pool building, but I would make it an all-adult or an all-family building. Have you ever heard the noise two four or five year. olds can make when they are frolicking in a pool? Ask a "day sleeper" tenant. He will tell you—as he is moving out his furniture.

So, if you have a pool, advertise it—"Pool."

If no pool, advertise it—"Quiet - no pool."

Chapter XXIV

PETS

or

"but mine is housebroken"

I was wrong when I said that a pool can cause the most problems—pets are much worse. But the reason I wasn't really wrong is that I have a pool and am stuck with it, but I don't have any pets in my buildings.

Did you ever live in an apartment building that allowed pets? I did! One tenant invariably has a dog that misses his master so he barks and cries, but never a whimper when master is home. This tenant would go out "on the town" and return at 3:15 a.m. I and all the other tenants knew it was 3:15 because that's when Fido would stop whining. So whenever this tenant stayed out late, I had to stay up late and watch the LATE LATE SHOW. Finally one of us had to give up—so I moved.

I must admit that I inherited pets in every building I ever purchased. But after a few months (and more than a few new carpets) I managed to get all my buildings free of all pets.

In one building we found ten cats living in, plus a few more regular boarders who were living out. It wasn't funny. I did not appreciate the neighborhood referring to my pride of ownership building as the "Cat House." I did not evict one single cat. I advised all tenants that the cats they now had were to be listed in the rental agreement, and that no more pets were to be allowed. I did not raise their rents. I did not raise their damage deposits because the damage was already done. But I did insist that no one was to leave water or food on the landings for stray boarders, and I guess that is what did it.

On the other hand, if you will accept pets you will never have a vacancy. You can immediately fill up any building if you will advertise "PETS ALLOWED." Some owners, in desperation because of two or three prolonged vacancies, have allowed pets in the vacant apartments. Two or three months later there are pets in every apartment. How can you say *no* to an old tenant when you say *yes* to a new tenant. And don't kid yourself—you might easily get an extra $100 damage deposit from a new tenant because of a pet, but try and get it from your present tenants. You can't, and you won't.

I know of a 100 unit townhouse cluster of buildings with three swimming pools with spacious grounds and beautiful lawns and landscaping. One tenant, in defiance of the pet restrictions, got a miniature poodle which was so small it could hardly be noticed by the managers. In fact, for the first few weeks the tenant toted the pup in and out of the building in her purse or a shopping bag. But other tenants' children were quick to notice and soon other dogs moved in, and the lawns began to be dug up. By the time the manager realized what was happening over 50% of the apartments had pets and the tenants, as if organized, dared the manager to evict them.

He was powerless, for the project was for sale and the sellers did not want vacancies on a large scale. So the grounds went to pot and, interestingly, the same "pet tenants" began to complain that the buildings were not being maintained properly anymore. They blamed it on management because the building was for sale; and it kept getting worse as the gardeners could not keep up with the natural habits of the cats and dogs. So a beautiful complex became an eyesore. Tenants without pets moved out because of the pets; and tenants with pets moved out because the project was getting run down. Here again is a plus for my argument that I prefer two or three small buildings to one large building. If this were a 10 unit building and one tenant violated the agreement by getting a dog, it would be difficult to keep the manager in the dark. This would be dealt with before it became a problem.

If you wish to know how to operate a "Pet Allowed" apartment building, you'll have to ask someone else since, I confess, I don't know how.

Chapter XXV

TV AERIALS

or

keep cats off your hot tin roof

Good TV reception is obviously a must. Color TV is here to stay, yet the building you bought is equipped only for black and white. Perhaps some tenants climbed onto the roof a couple of years ago and put up their own color antenna. And when they moved some climbed up again and removed the antenna and some did not.

Look at the jungle of aerials. No one knows which goes where. In the meanwhile, most of the tenants are getting adequate reception. Only one or two complain but you can always tell them it must be their set, because all the other tenants get good reception. Finally, one adventurous tenant climbs onto the roof (you will be sued if he falls off), puts up his own private antenna with the lead wire hanging over the side of the building and coming into his bedroom through a window screen that he has punched a hole through. My month-to-month agreement forbids such installation but all the TV "trees" were planted before I took over.

The problem won't go away and you will soon need a re-roofing job if you let your tenants walk all over your roof. I found three ceiling leaks directly attributable to three amateurish antenna installations in one building—two of them were not even hooked up to an apartment.

You don't know anything about the type of aerials or the condition, so get a professional to take them all down and put up a master aerial system with color and UHF. Do this as soon as you take over for it will improve the appearance of the building and the "Movie of the Week" reception. The cost is negligible compared to the importance of this rehabilitation.

And always advise the tenants what you are doing—and why. The following letter will show you how this is done:

August 7, 19XX

Next week, we plan to remove all TV antennas from the roof as we have no way of knowing who is hooked up to color or UHF.

We will install a new Master system which will give everyone the best reception possible whether black and white; color; or UHF.

Every apartment has a TV outlet in the living room and this will be hooked-up to the new Master antenna at no cost to you, of course.

If you also wish another hook-up (such as a bedroom) this can be arranged at a nominal charge to you of $10 if done at the same time. If so, please advise the Manager.

On the day of installation there will be a slight interruption of TV reception.

Thank you for your cooperation.

Sincerely,

Joseph Schwartz

Chapter XXVI

WHAT KIND OF INSURANCE?

or

keeping under cover

No need to remind you that you should have fire insurance on the building. The mortgagor will make certain of that and will usually take care of it through an insurance agency that they own. Here again I am resentful of the pressure to place business in affiliated companies. I always insist on using my own insurance agent. No lender dare object but they will make it sound much simpler if they can place the fire insurance. And the subtle implication that the deal will close much faster usually works as their captive insurance agency's volume would tend to indicate. However, if you do not have your own insurance man then you should let the mortgagor take care of it for you.

Any general insurance agency can also provide the liability coverage that you should have. Be sure you carry maximum coverage. The additional cost for $1,000,000 coverage is relatively low compared to $100,000. If in doubt, discuss the coverages needed with your Apartment House Association.

There are two insurance needs that most amateur apartment house owners do not have covered—and the lack of either of them can bankrupt you. The first one is Workmen's Compensation. Even though your manager is only getting a $50 reduction in rent, if he breaks his neck falling off a ladder while replacing a light bulb, you will be liable. Your manager is working for you—minor as to work but major as to liability. So make certain that he or anyone else who claims to be performing any work for you is covered by Workmen's Compensation. In some states there is a state operated Workmen's Compensation insurance company. In every state there are minimum benefits required to be provided by every employer. And a $40 or $50 reduction in rent makes you an employer.

The second important insurance most often neglected is the "Non-Owned Auto." If your manager is driving his car to the hardware store to buy some light bulbs and he is involved in an accident, you might be liable because he was at work for you. In fact, even if he was not on a mission for you, anyone might claim he was, and might sue you because they know he is your manager and you have more assets than he has.

Non-Owned Auto coverage is often overlooked, perhaps because the premium is so nominal that the insurance companies and the agents neglect to solicit it.

I have $500,000 bodily injury and property damage Employer's Non-Ownership Automobile Liability protection for an extra annual premium of $19 a year. It can be added to your apartment building liability policy—INSIST ON IT.

Note: Again I have erred. The $19 annual premium quoted above is wrong. In fairness to the insurance company, may I change it to read "an extra annual premium of $19 per year FOR ALL THREE BUILDINGS." So now you can appreciate why your insurance agent might not write or phone you for a $6.33 annual premium. He can't afford to. But you can write or phone him—for you cannot afford not to. And if he's never heard of Non-Owned Auto coverage, find an agent who has.

Chapter XXVII

THE BUILDING PLANS

or

there ought to be a law

All builders should be required by law to furnish all building plans to the owner, and the owner who sells a building should be required, in turn, to furnish to the buyer the original building plans plus any plans of major alterations.

I cannot understand the disregard shown by the builder and architect after a building has once been completed and approved as meeting the city's building code. The plans disappear as if on purpose; and I truly believe that in many cases, it is on purpose.

I could not get the plans for any one of my three apartment buildings, but I sure tried. I went to the City Building

Department where I secured copies of the original permits but I was told that all plans submitted to them were destroyed one year after the permit was finally approved. The permits did give me the names of the engineers, architects, and builders, but no names of plumbing or electrical contractors. Two of the three builders had gone bankrupt, one engineer was dead (his successor had no plans), and one architect had moved East. Despite my offer to pay, I could find no involved person who had a copy of the plans.

Even on a five story office building only four years old, no building plans were made available. I was finally able to secure a copy of the plans from the architect but they were practically useless because they were not on an "as built" basis. In other words, as the construction progressed many changes were made, but the architect, in this case, had no responsibility beyond the original drawings. The original plumbing, air-conditioning, electrical, and elevator plans had to be submitted for approval by the City Building Department, and then the changes had to be resubmitted. For the proper maintenance of an office building, "as built" plans are of inestimable value to the owner. Yet they were not available. So I am serious in suggesting that all building construction plans should be required to be retained by law. And if this should become law, you will have to thank your Apartment Association for they are the ones who will sponsor such legislation. In fact, I wish to acknowledge that my local association had this under consideration prior to the date of this writing.

However, any such law will not help me in relation to the buildings I now own for it cannot be made retroactive. I was determined to find a way to get such plans as I find essential to operate my buildings more efficiently.

I phoned a nearby college and asked whether they included architecture as one of their courses of study. They did not, but they referred me to another college that did. I phoned the second school and asked for the head of the architectural department. I told him of my problem and he agreed immediately that this was a problem common to the majority of "my size" apartment building owners. My suggestion that students might find this type of project helpful in their studies and money-wise, also was of interest to the Professor.

So we arranged to meet to discuss the project in detail. When we met, the Prof told me that he had already discussed my call with members of his staff and with a group of students and everyone agreed that we should explore the subject.

Note: Years ago I had come to the realization that, as is often stated, there is no such thing as a "new idea." However, I also realized that very few people follow through on their thoughts. I offer my "follow-through" in the hope that it may be useful to at least a few of the 7,500,000 rental unit owners (of less than 50 units in size).

It is difficult, time-consuming, and expensive to attempt to get a complete set of architectural drawings, including elevations, structural specifications, plumbing, electrical, etc. In fact, it is impossible, for you need the talents of engineers and plumbing and electrical contractors in addition to the architect. Ironically, all of these professions were engaged in the construction of the building and all had submitted drawings for approval.

So the Professor and I agreed we were not talking of complete structural plans, not even complete architectural plans, for we were not going to expect a student or a college to attempt to compete in the area that is served by the architectural firms. We had to come up with a simple set of specifications that would be meaningful to the owner of the building and which the professional architect would not consider as a transgression. In fact, we should even have a non-competitive simple term to apply to these specifications rather than refer to them as building plans or architectural drawings.

I had the audacity to act as spokesman for the 7½ million, and set the specifications as follows:

No exterior drawings—

> the owner knows what the building looks like and he can always borrow a Polaroid.

Apartment interiors only—

> measurements of every room, wall, window, closet, bathroom and kitchen fixture (in relation to every room of each apartment, and in relation to each apartment to every other apartment), all of this in the form of drawings to scale.

I also concocted a name for our project—Architectural Student Interior Schematics (AS-IS drawings).

Project AS-IS is underway (see letter and drawing that follow) and when completed I can stop guessing. I will know!

December 13, 19XX

Dear Friend:

In conjunction with three architectural students, I am participating in a new project. We are going to be the initiators of having scale drawings made of every apartment -- called:

Architectural Students Interior Schematics (AS-IS)

In order to complete the drawings, it will be necessary to measure every room in your apartment. No furniture need be moved and this requires no preparation on your part whatsoever.

The date is Tuesday, December 18. If you will not be able to be present I request permission to take the gentlemen through your apartment.

We will not need more than 30 minutes in an apartment, and we will be responsible, as either I, or the Manager will be present throughout every measuring session.

Thank you for your cooperation.

Sincerely,

Joseph Schwartz

NOTE: Thought you might be interested -- this project is expected to create much needed part-time work for architectural students throughout the country. Also possible credits towards their course requirements -- and I am proud to be the originator of the program and its name.

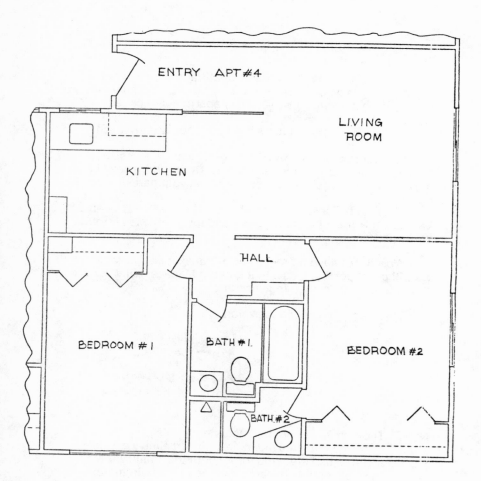

Chapter XXVIII

SECURITY BUILDING

or

ain't no such

Perhaps one of my reasons for preferring smaller buildings is because of security. I believe they are more secure from uninvited "company."

A large building is usually three or more stories high, with elevators, with underground parking, but more important, with inside halls. Every one of these features is an invitation to the prowler. The elevator is the worst possible place to meet up with a mugger; the underground parking, even though barred and locked, is a preferred playground for the common thug; and the inside halls are the door-lock-picker's dream.

I won't even consider a *small* building with inside halls. All "my size" buildings (in Southern California) are garden-type buildings. Garden-type does not mean there must be a garden. There might be only a concrete court, but if there is a garden, I guess it means that all doors open out onto the garden (or court) area. Or, as I like to describe my buildings, every front door opens outside to the open air and not to an enclosed hallway. Therefore, every front door can be seen from the garden or court. A prowler is stupid to go from door-to-door at any of my buildings. And since many apparently are not stupid, I have never had one burglary attempt on any of my apartments.

A high-rise next to one of my buildings has had a number of break-ins. The next morning, my tenants (and I) affirm once again that our little garden-type building with no locked gates, with no doors with buzzer let-inners, is much more secure than the so-called full security building.

Chapter XXIX

NOISE POLLUTION

or

uppers vs. lowers

This year about 29% of the apartment dwellers will move (according to a nation-wide survey). Many of the moves will be due to NOISE (according to my one-man survey).

There are building noises, and there are tenant noises. Some can be solved and some are hopeless. But before anyone generalizes and condemns all apartment living as a noisy existence, ask the private home owner who has the misfortune of having a noisy next-door neighbor who doesn't give a damn for *his* next-door neighbor. At least the apartment tenant can move.

135

Being aware of the noise problem I will not buy any building where the second floor is plywood. You can't see it because it is always carpeted, but you can hear it squeak. The tenant in the lower is so annoyed by the squeaky floors above that his next move is sure to be to an upper in another building.

My buildings' top floors have carpeting over either hardwood or elastizill (latter is a 1¾ inch layer of cellular concrete which is both a fire and sound deterrent). Result—no squeaks. I also have insulated walls which help reduce noise but is of little use against an unreasonable neighbor.

Every landlord and tenant is aware of TV and stereo 11 P.M. rules, but what about the bedroom TV against the wall which has the headboard of the neighbors bed on the other side of the same wall. This is easily resolved by requesting that no TV's be against any common wall.

The indelicate subject of "going to the bathroom" is never discussed, for the landlord and the agreement only go as far as the garbage disposal and the dishwasher. Yet the bathroom plumbing is the noisiest noise of all. You can do nothing to solve it—but your tenants can, and will. All "down under" tenants know the toilet and shower habits of their "uppers," even in the Holiday Inn. And if the upstairs tenant is aware of this, you'd be surprised how quickly it is resolved. I agree that you cannot ask a person whether he needs to use the toilet in the middle of the night. He would think you were a nut—and you would be. But suppose you just nonchalantly show the new "upper" the rules that follow. I haven't even mentioned "toilet," but they get the point. And not one person has ever been offended by these reasonable suggestions.

SENSIBLE, CONSIDERATE, NEIGHBORLY RULES

1. In consideration of others—after 11 P.M. and before 9 A.M.—typing, singing, playing a musical instrument, loud operation of TV, stereo, radio, or unnecessary noises or boisterous conduct is not permitted if disturbing to any other tenant.

2. Garbage disposals, dishwashers, showers and bath tubs are very noisy and cannot be soundproofed against. Please do not use the disposal or dishwasher after 11 P.M. And if taking a bath or shower during "usual sleeping hours," please run the water at a very low pressure. Your neighbor will appreciate this unusual consideration—and so would you if you lived "down under." FOR A FULL BLAST SHOWER OR TUB IS UNBEARABLY NOISY, EVEN IN THE HILTON (or in Las Vegas, when the guy upstairs comes in at 3 A.M. and takes a 30-minute shower, all you can do is dress, go to the lobby, and lose again).

I developed my "Sensible, Considerate and Neighborly Rules" because of the following incident. I had an upstairs tenant who used to shower every night for over 30 minutes, full force, after the Johnny Carson show. As the "down under" tenant turned in his keys for his key deposit, he told me that I should rent the vacancy to people who were deaf—and he told me why. I stayed up that night and watched Johnny to the bitter end and then I went into the vacant apartment and thought I was at the Niagara Falls without my ear plugs. I never would have believed the racket that an upstairs shower could cause in a downstairs bedroom wall. If any real estate agent had called on me at that hour, he would have gotten a listing on that building—and at a low figure.

The next day I called on the "showerer." With a 30-day

notice in my pocket, I hesitantly and embarrassingly explained the reason for my call. He didn't believe me—so we turned on his shower and went downstairs. I fully expected the tenant to tell me to go to hell. What right do I have to tell a guy that he cannot take a shower whenever he wishes? To my surprise, when he heard the awful noise he apologized and said he wished the tenant who moved had spoken to him about it. He had no idea the shower was annoying anyone, and he added that he could just as well shower earlier in the evening. He is still my tenant. (I'll give him a free copy of this book so he won't sue me for invasion of privacy.)

In another building, I inherited a Saturday and Sunday door-open full volume stereo blaster. The seller and the manager both told me that he would not cooperate by turning the volume down but persisted in disturbing the entire building. I knew he had to go, so once again I made a call with the 30-day notice in my pocket. You won't believe what I learned. He had never once been asked by anyone, owner, manager, or tenant, to turn down the volume. In fact, since he had a very expensive stereo set with a most valuable collection of classical recordings, he was under the impression that the tenants enjoyed the concerts he provided every week-end. End of public concerts.

These are people problems and you can deal with reasonable people. You can also prevent many people problems from ever happening. I will not accept a tenant who has a motorcycle or a souped-up triple-muffler car. I will not accept a night-worker day-sleeper in a family building with children. I will not accept a rock and roll musician if he plans to have rehearsals in his apartment. And when any of the kids in my building take up the trumpet they had better use a mute, or I will once again make a call with the 30-day notice in my pocket.

Chapter XXX

P: S:

or

products & services

As soon as you buy an apartment building you are also a buyer of carpets, drapes, garbage disposals, light bulbs; and an employer of painters, plumbers, carpet shampooers, window washers, carpenters and, most important of all, a handyman.

Don't let the above intimidate you. It's fun. You contribute to our economy; you spend money; and you make money.

Apartment building ownership is a stable investment not comparable to shares of stock. You never know the value of your stocks—one day it is up, the next day it is down. But your building is always worth more. The value of any properly operated building is "the amount you paid plus a profit."

Proper operation means that you *do not*—I repeat—you *do not* shop for carpeting each time you need to recarpet an apartment. You not only know the price, the color, the quality, but you also know where you buy it—today—and that it will be installed tomorrow.

There are carpet dealers who deal exclusively with apartment buildings. Find one before you need him. Your apartment house association will supply you with a list of reputable firms. Visit one or two and decide on the color and grade. Standardize. Do not use avocado green in one apartment and gold in another. Stay with one color and one grade and you will save time and money. If one year after recarpeting, the living room or a bedroom carpet has been damaged, you can recarpet that one room, for you are using a standard always-in-stock brand of carpet.

The same applies to drapes. Use one supplier for all your drapery needs. You will thus be assured that whether you need only one small drape, or an entire apartment redraped, you will get good service at a fair price and they will match.

Painting will be the service most often needed. Choose one neutral color of one large paint manufacturer, and paint all apartments the same. (Any color is good as long as it is white.) And use the same painting contractor; one who specializes in apartments. Believe me, there is a tremendous difference in using the specialist. I know, for I have done it both ways. The non-specialist takes two days to do a job that the specialist does in a *half day*, at half the cost, and the specialist does a better job because he knows you are a perpetual customer.

Even such a simple thing as cleaning of drapes can be the most annoying, time-consuming and costly chore of all. Every owner has tried the obvious method of cleaning drapes—he has used the laundromat (after all, the drapes are washable). The drapes shrink or come out shredded and the laundromat isn't responsible. Find the professional apartment drape cleaner who will take down the drapes and deliver and hang them up again. Costs you more, but costs you less. Many owners will not agree with me because they will say that their managers take down the drapes, remove all the pins, take them to the laundromat or the corner cleaner, pick them up, insert the pins, and hang up the drapes. I say that even though the drapes might come through safe and clean, the time consumed by the manager is not warranted for the few dollars saved.

A handyman is a "jack of all trades" and he will save you plenty of "Jack." It is easy to get the big jobs done such as a $2,000 reroofing job, but try to get a roofer for a $25 or $50 patch job. The small jobs, such as repairing a screen door, or replacing one light fixture, or replacing the innards of a toilet tank—for these problems you need a small job specialist. Your local newspaper's classified section is the handyman's exclusive form of advertising. Line one up the day before you take over a building because you are going to need him the day after.

Note: Before you replace a ventilating fan motor, or replace a sticky sliding window, or replace a balky lock, or buy a new electric razor—just give them each a squirt of WD-40. I don't know what WD-40 is made of, but it's a miracle performer. If you don't believe me, watch any maintenance man—but watch him closely because when he thinks you're not looking he'll give anything he can't fix a squirt of WD-40. I have no business connection with WD-40. In fact, I have not asked for permission to include this product in my book. At least they should buy a copy.

So all I have said in this chapter can be summed up by these few words: Standardize on one product and one supplier.

But I cannot end this chapter as to services without adding

a few words about an unusual stand-by service that every apartment operator should be prepared to furnish. A large electric fan and a good sized electric heater should be always on hand. When an air conditioner doesn't function it isn't the fault of the tenant and it never occurs except in the heat of the summer. Why shouldn't the landlord be prepared to lend the tenant the use of a circulating electric fan? Or when the heater doesn't function (always on a cold day), why not supply an electric heater to let the tenant know that he has a landlord who cares?

Chapter XXXI

CONDOMINIUMS AHEAD?

or

no need to panic

The hue and cry throughout the country is "CONDOMIN-IUMS." Many apartment building owners are fearful that rentals will soon be passe. I assure you the opportunities for knowledgeable landlords have never been greater than now—and will even be greater in the condominium's future.

The newly built condominiums cannot be competitive with the ten year old apartments, unless the condominium is way outside the city in the boon-docks (where there are no ten year old apartments anyway).

Condominiums cannot be built today at yesterday's costs— and today's costs for urban area development seems to require a sales price of $30 to $50 a square foot. Apartment buildings, with much less "ersatz" building materials than today's condos, can be purchased for less than $20 a square foot— well-constructed, insulated, larger rooms, in closer-in seasoned locations. So the rent paid for a comparable apartment can be less than the *net cost* (after taxes and principal payments) of a condominium, and many people have already discovered this to be so.

It is difficult to generalize when we have such a vast country with so many factors affecting costs, and so many location-variables with land values commanding prices of from $2 a foot to no limit whatsoever. How can one generalize when condominiums vary from $19,999 to $150,000?

I found a tremendous difference in costs when I was asked for my opinion of a condominium project in Massachusetts a few weeks after I had checked one in California for a pro-spective buyer. And both buyers bought, so I am not anti-condominium. But the difference between the two condos was unbelievable. In Massachusetts, I found 2 bedrooms, one bath, 1,000 square feet, no garage or carport (just 2 outdoor car spaces), no community swimming pool or community anything. In California, it was 4 bedrooms, 3 bathrooms (one full, one ¾ and one ½), 2,000 square feet, double car garage attached, community swimming pool and beautiful com-munity "Town Hall" where all the members can attend their management and assessment meetings.

The Massachusetts condo sold for $39,950. The California condo sold for $43,500. However, the Massachusetts property was two short blocks from a beautiful public ocean beach front and was built on land that I would guess cost about $15 to $20 a square foot. The California property was about 25 miles from the city, on rocky, sandy, desolate land that I estimate cost the developers about $2 to $3 a square foot.

Both buyers had been renters of apartments at a cost less than the projected net cost for their condos. The condo advantage apparently in both of these cases was the appeal of ownership.

What does this prove? I believe it proves that condominiums will be an increasingly important factor in housing but their main competition will be with the ownership of individual houses rather than apartment rentals, for thousands upon thousands of people prefer to rent because of mobility.

Young people usually are not yet established in their employment to be able to settle down on a permanent basis in a fixed location, so they prefer the freedom of rentals.

Older people have already had a single home. Their children are grownup and Grandma is tired of preparing the Thanksgiving Dinner for their kids and their kids' kids. The old folks have reached the age where they welcome the "irresponsibility" of a one bedroom apartment. And from then on they get invited to their oldest daughter's home for Thanksgiving, for Grandpa's apartment is too small—and for that, Grandma "gives thanks."

That leaves us with a lot of middle-aged people, many of whom are living in their very own single residence with a yard and a lawn to care for. They read the condo ads and they are attracted by the advantage that appeals most to them—no lawn to care for.

So the apartment house owner has a vast market among the young, the old, and also many of the middle-aged (until the latter group gets the urge as the Massachusetts and California couples did).

There is another very interesting, widely advertised

campaign of condominium promotional activity. I refer to the intense solicitation of present apartment building owners to "convert to condominiums" and make a fortune. This, in my opinion, will phase out to a mere trickle as it is neither practical nor even possible for the majority of buildings to be so converted. I recently attended a "Convert Your Apartment Building To a Condominium" seminar with an imposing array of attorneys, engineer/architects, and condominium conversion experts. The speakers were excellent and most candid in their discourses, even to the point of telling the audience the amount of their fees for their services (and they were substantial). But the projections of the profits of conversion made the fees seem quite inconsequential. After a couple of hours I was impelled to ask a question, preceded by the following:

"The building code dictates the minimum number of parking spaces required for apartment buildings. It used to be one for one—and my three buildings have exactly one car space for each apartment and there is no space to be found for additional cars. In the past few years we know that the code for urban areas has been changed to 1¼ and 1½ car spaces per unit and all new apartment buildings must comply with this increased parking space requirement. And I even understand that the trend is to raise it to two car spaces per unit. Now my question is—in converting to condominiums, do existing apartment buildings have to comply with the increased parking space requirements?"

The answer was "Yes. Your building would be subject to the present parking requirements if you were to try to get a permit for the condominiums."

I answered, "If that is the case, then none of my buildings would qualify and I doubt that many buildings represented here would qualify."

At that point another person in the audience spoke up and asked:

"Did you say that all present buildings must have parking spaces to comply with the new requirements?"

The speaker answered "Yes, I did."

Thereupon the questioner stated: "I agree with the other gentleman. My apartment buildings could not possibly comply and, therefore, I don't understand what this big to-do is all about. I don't think anyone in this audience owns an apartment building that could comply."

And this is why I claim that this campaign to convert existing apartment buildings to condominiums will phase out since I doubt that 5% of the buildings (only those built in the past three or four years) could comply with the present parking requirements.

Therefore, in conclusion, I wish to emphasize that the additional parking requirements and the continued inflation must cause the sale price of new condominiums to be ever increasing—likewise increasing the value of your existing apartment building.

If you have observed the "exterior" and "location" rules of this book, and you treat your "tenants as customers," you need have no fear about your investment in an apartment building.

EPILOGUE

The day I air-mailed the corrected galleys to my publisher, my wife asked, "Were you serious when you wrote in your book that you were going to buy a 4th and a 5th building?"

"Sure I was serious—but I didn't say when. I'll run across another building someday."

"Well, if you meant it," continued my wife, "then you'd better get busy. After your book is released, thousands of readers in this area will be looking for exactly the same buildings you want. You will be competing with readers who will want to buy—and many who are now owners will no longer want to sell their property. So I think you had better buy while you can."

When my wife is right—she is!

So this is to announce that I am no longer a three building owner of 28 units—the score is now four buildings totaling 41 units. And I have already made an offer on a fifth.

When I told this to my publisher, he said, "Joe, you must have read your own book."

I did. And I'm pleased to report the first satisfied customer.

INDEX

151

— NOTES —

— NOTES —

— NOTES -

— NOTES —

— NOTES —

— NOTES —